William Bright

Hymns and other Poems

William Bright

Hymns and other Poems

ISBN/EAN: 9783744776592

Printed in Europe, USA, Canada, Australia, Japan

Cover: Foto ©Thomas Meinert / pixelio.de

More available books at **www.hansebooks.com**

To the Clergy

OF

ST. JOHN BAPTIST'S, OXFORD,

IN GRATEFUL REMEMBRANCE

OF THE

PRIVILEGES OF YEARS.

CONTENTS.

	PAGE
DOMINE, Refugium	1
Morning Hymn	7
Evening Hymn	10
Easter Communion	13
Christmas Communion	16
Eucharistic Comfort	18
At the Holy Eucharist	20
"We have an Altar"	22
After Communion	24
"Ye are come unto Mount Sion"	26
The Sympathies of Christ	30
"Ubi Charitas et Amor"	34
Hymn for the Close of a Service	36
Hymn before a Journey	38

CONTENTS.

	PAGE
Hymn for Passion-tide	41
Hymn for Michaelmas	44
Hymn for a Martyr's Day	49
An Intercession	55
Acts of Prayer	58
Temptation	60
Penitence	63
Prayer after Pardon	65
Tribulation and Wealth	67
Patience	71
Thankfulness	75
A Perfect Heart	79
Zeal	82
Hiding from God	85
The Corner Stone, a Stumbling Stone	89
St. Martin's Vision	93
Secular Opinion	97
The Greatness of Common Life	100
Hell	103
Antichrist	106
The Atonement	110
The Priesthood	114
The Evening Absolution	117
Ritual	120
St. Tudno's	124

CONTENTS.

	PAGE
The "Angelus" at Lucerne	128
St. Gervais, Rouen	133
The Scillitan Martyrs	139
The Vision of Saturus	145
St. Fructuosus	149
Theodore of Antioch	156
The Battle of Varna	162
A Tradition of Culloden	167
Louis the Seventeenth	170
The Odyssey, I. 1—95	177

ERRATA.

Page 121, line 15, erase the hyphen.
„ 123, transpose ; and , at the end of the third and fourth lines of the last stanza.
„ 165, last line but one, for 'aid' read 'aid?'

And all hollow faiths to nought ;
O what doubts, what drear negations,
Straightway 'neath our feet are trod,
When we answer with our Credo
In a true and living God !

Domine, Refugium.

THOU hast been, Thou art our Refuge,
   When this day of surging thought
Brings all sanctities to question,
   And all hollow faiths to nought;
O what doubts, what drear negations,
   Straightway 'neath our feet are trod,
When we answer with our Credo
   In a true and living God!

Not a name for boundless Nature,
　Not a blind mechanic Cause,
Not a sum of vital forces,
　Not a slave of iron laws;
Not an abdicated Ruler,
　Who could once a world create,
Then leave all His will had fashioned
　To a self-evolving fate:

But a God that acts and governs,
　Now, as on Creation's day;
Love's most special care combining
　With His widest general sway;
One whose grand continuous fiat
　Every moment props the spheres,
One who bends His whole omniscience
　On each new-made orphan's tears.

Yes—a real Guide and Father,
 Yes—a real Judge and Lord ;
Whose perpetual moral presence
 Round our deepest life is poured ;
One who verily can love us,
 Hear our cry, and make us blest ;
Who ordains His deepest witness
 In the voice within our breast.

· But full surely He would give us
 Clearer tokens of His will,
And our need to touch Him closer
 He would, Father-like, fulfil :
So to powers and laws transcendent
 Nature's outward course might yield,
And our own God shine before us,
 In His wealth of grace revealed.

Therefore men that read the story
   Of the Manger and the Rood,
Well may greet the only Gospel
   Straight from Him, the only Good :
Heart and mind go forth to meet it,
   This is light, or light is none,
To believe in God the Father
   And in Jesus Christ His Son.

This is light ;—where dimness lingers,
   Faith can wait till shadows flee ;
And Life's riddles less perplex us
   When the Truth has made us free ;
Yea, the Truth and Light Incarnate—
   For if Christ we truly scan,
Him we trust in we must worship,
   Word made Flesh, and God made Man.

Nought but this, the living fulness
    Of His own Emmanuel Name,
Links His human truth and pureness
    With the splendours of His claim;
He that took His sovereign station
    Where no Angel durst come nigh,
Would be neither Saint nor Prophet
    Were He less than God most high.

But we know Thee, O good Jesus!
    And Thy words are life indeed;
And Thine own all-glorious Person
    Gives coherence to our Creed:
Strong in that majestic oneness,
    Each high doctrine holds its place;
Each a ground of holy action
    And a pledge of constant grace.

DOMINE, REFUGIUM.

Take then, Lord, our prostrate worship,
    Take our best of thanks and praise,
For the dear, dear love that keeps us
    From the doubter's woeful ways;
Though the strife of tongues be with us,
    On our thoughts imprint Thy sign;
Till all questions find their answer
    In that life where all is Thine.

Morning Hymn.

TO thank Thee, Lord, for this new morn
   We come before Thy face ;
Make Thou the hours till eventide
   A perfect day of grace.

We know, to bless our common life,
   Thou hast a precept given,
That we, redeemed, should walk on earth
   As citizens of heaven.

But, Father! well Thou know'st that oft
    We find the world too strong;
That powers at deadly war with Faith
    Around our pathway throng.

When things of sense their claim assert
    With such a royal mien,
'Tis hard to keep all homage back
    For majesties unseen.

Men feel no awe for verities
    Whose voice is soft and still;
They thrust aside the realm of Grace—
    It lets them have their will.

Self-hardened towards diviner things,
    Each day they own them less;
While through their being steals the plague
    Of utter worldliness.

O keep us, Lord, from such a doom !
O grant us power and love
What lies before us here to do,
But fix our hearts above.

Amid the transient, make us true
To that which knows no end;
Let holy thoughts and acts of faith
With earthly business blend :

So shall the beauty of our God *
Beam o'er us all the day;
And this poor handiwork be rich
In fruits that ne'er decay.

Evening Hymn.

 GOD, in this calm eventide
   Let two great thoughts with us abide;
How dust shall unto dust return,
And how Thy love doth o'er us yearn.

The days of man are but as grass;
They spring, they flourish, and they pass;
But to the faithful and the pure
Thy mercy stands for ever sure.

O joy for them! they well may brook
With fearless eyes on death to look;
Their spirit makes its firm abode
In that paternal heart of God.

Enthroned in all-sufficing rest,
He still desires to see us blest;
As mother comforts darling son *,
So bends He o'er us, one by one.

Full oft this day His pardon sweet
Has sped from far, some child to meet;
Has welcomed home the lost and found,
And made His Heaven with joy resound.

Thy power, O Lord, reveals Thee less
Than glimpses of Thy tenderness;

* Isa. lxvi. 13.

EVENING HYMN.

And we, though here we know in part,
May write " He loves me " on our heart.

So pass we on from day to day,
With strength to work and will to pray,
And two things certain—We must die,
And—Thou wouldst have us live on high.

Easter Communion.*

THOU that on the first of Easters
Cam'st resplendent from the tomb,
Leaving all Thy linen cerements
Folded in the cavern's gloom,
Come with Thine "All hail" to greet us,
Come our Paschal joy to be;
Let our Altar, clad in brightness,
Yield a throne of white for Thee.

---

* Reprinted in substance from the "Lyra Eucharistica," edited by the Rev. O. Shipley.

This shall crown the Queen of Sundays;
  Grant but this, our cup runs o'er;
Peal on peal of Alleluias
  Makes us long for this the more.
Faces bright with Easter gladness
  Yet their joy's perfection crave
In the glorious Paschal banquet
  Of the King that spoiled the grave.

Thou whose all-transcendent Manhood
  Knew not aught of bonds imposed,
Rising ere the stone was lifted,
  Passing where the doors were closed;
Thou whose name is still the Wondrous,
  Is there aught too hard for Thee?
Let Thy dread and blissful Presence
  From our evils make us free.

EASTER COMMUNION.

Agnus Dei! we are guilty;
    Panis Vitæ! we are faint;
But Thou didst not rise at Easter
    To be deaf to our complaint.
Come, O come to cleanse and feed us,
    Breathing peace and kindling love,
Till Thy Paschal blessings bear us
    To the Feast of feasts above.

Christmas Communion.[*]

T last Thou art come! and the dew of Thy birth
Is the fragrance of heaven to Thy pilgrims on earth;
All life at Thy coming grows radiant and sweet,
And our very hearts' homage we lay at Thy feet;
Though worthless our best, let us do what we can
To welcome Thy birthday, true God and true Man.

O light to our eyes, and O life to our heart,
Can words ever tell what a Saviour Thou art,
Who to ransom our souls, and to fill us with good,
Didst stoop to the Manger, the Garden, the Rood?

[*] Reprinted from the "Lyra Eucharistica."

Take our thanks unexpressed, while adoring we fall
In Thine own very Presence, our God and our All.

For us Thou wast born, Thou didst die, Thou dost
    live ;
Our praise Thou canst perfect, our sin canst forgive ;
That want lies the deepest ; 'tis mercy we need,
And the souls Thou absolvest keep Christmas indeed :
Let the touch of Thy Manhood our cleansing renew,
And Thy deep Heart of love to itself make us true.

When in hearts that once hailed Thee the gladness
    dies out,
When lips that adored Thee now question and doubt,
When they half deem it gain from Thy yoke to be
    free,
O grant us to cleave all the closer to Thee !
That if others draw back, we may do what we can
To live for Thy service, true God and true Man.

Eucharistic Comfort.*

AWFUL might of Grace Divine,
   That can our shallow thoughts reprove,
And in the simplest forms enshrine
   Such heights and depths and worlds of love!
Yea, all God's mercies earthward sent
Are in the Blessed Sacrament.

For we have all, if we have Thee,
   Who giv'st us here Thy Flesh and Blood,
And giv'st us faith withal to see
   That miracle of ghostly food;

* Reprinted from the "Lyra Eucharistica."

To her keen eyes the veil is rent
That shrouds the Blessed Sacrament.

With her we lift our hearts on high,
   By self condemned, by God forgiven ;
. With her to Jesus we draw nigh,
   And stretch our hands for Bread from heaven ;
No more in sin's foul dungeon pent,
We touch the Blessed Sacrament.

" It is the Lord !" no thought but this
   Can compass all our wondrous gain ;
" It is the Lord," our Life, our Bliss,
   Who died, who lives to plead and reign,
And whose vast love has fullest vent
In this most Blessed Sacrament.

At the Holy Eucharist.

LORD, we bid Thee welcome,
    Filled with love and awe ;
Though the heavens contain Thee
    After nature's law,
Yet, as all the faithful
    Share that Heart of Thine,
So Thy Body findeth
    Here a mystic shrine.

Take our worthless homage,
    O Thou Prince of Peace ;
In this boon transcendent
    Still our faith increase ;

AT THE HOLY EUCHARIST.

May our lips confess it
    Till our latest breath,
May it light our passage
    Through the gates of death.

Here, although we see not,
    Yet we trust Thy word;
But the full fruition—
    Grant it, grant it, Lord *!
O to gaze upon Thee
    Without a veil like this,
When to see Thy glory
    Shall be all our bliss!

---

* See the Rhythmus of Aquinas.

"We have an Altar."

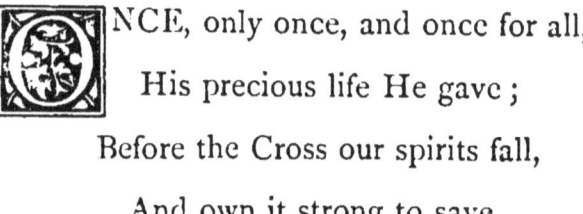NCE, only once, and once for all,
    His precious life He gave;
Before the Cross our spirits fall,
    And own it strong to save.

"One Offering, single and complete,"
    With lips and heart we say;
But what He never can repeat,
    He shows forth day by day.

For as the priest of Aaron's line
    Within the Holiest stood,
And sprinkled all the Mercy-shrine
    With sacrificial blood;

"WE HAVE AN ALTAR."

Our Priest and Victim, adding nought *
To His Atonement's power,
Presents Himself † for those He bought
In that dark noontide hour.

So pleads the Flesh that died and lives,
On Heaven's eternal throne,
And where in mystic rite He gives
Its Presence to His own.

And so we show Thy Death, O Lord,
Till Thou again appear;
And feel, when we approach Thy board,
We have an Altar here.

---

* See Dr. Pusey on Truth and Office of English Church, p. 28.
† Heb. ix. 24.

After Communion.[*]

HIS is the Feast that pleaseth Thee, O
Lord;
This is the Feast that Thou didst leave behind
For orphaned ones, in token of Thy love.
O Wisdom of the Father, Virgin-born,
O Thou who hast not deemed it too much grace
To let a worthless sinner touch and take
Thy sacred, precious Body; what reward
For all Thy bounties can I give to Thee?
For if the holy deeds of all the world
Were heaped together, they would show as nought
Beside Thy gracious goodness. Therefore now

[*] From an Ambrosian Missal of A.D. 1522.

AFTER COMMUNION.

I thank Thee, King of kings, and Lord of lords,
Son of the living God,—Lord Jesus Christ,
And far as these weak powers of mine can reach,
I render thanks to Thy dread majesty
And kindness infinite, O kindest Lord,
Who sweetly hast refreshed my dried-up soul
With Thy most holy Body and Thy Blood.
I pray Thee, Lord, that what in me is found
Faulty, and running counter to Thy will,
May wholly be uprooted, and my heart
Prepared to be the Spirit's meet abode.
And grant that this Communion, dearest Lord,
May to my soul be sweetness and delight,
In persecution and adversity
Be safety and protection, peace and joy
In trouble and temptation, light and strength
In every word and work, and confidence,
Comfort, and final tutelage, in death.

"We are come unto Mount Sion."

WHEN Heaven's high doors were lifted up,
    And, bright with many a royal crown *,
The Flesh that drained the Passion-cup
    In majesty of God sat down,
Then, then, O miracle of love!
    The gulf was bridged, the bars were riven,
And things below met things above,
    And earth was clasped in arms of Heaven.

So now to our true Sion height
    We in this mortal life are come;
E'en now we hail, by faith's pure light,
    The many mansions of our home:

* Rev. xix. 12.

E'en now, ere dust returns to dust,
    That far-spread host of Angel powers,
That concourse of the first-born just,
    In Christ, the Head of all, are ours.

If thus of old the Spirit taught,
    If thus we sing in daily Creed,
Then who from heaven hath tidings brought
    That Saints can take of us no heed;
That sympathies are quenched and chilled
    In souls from touch of sin set free,
In harboured ones that prayer is stilled
    For brethren tossed on this world's sea?

No—while the Lamb that once was slain
    Stands forth to take our sins away,
One impulse thrills the ransomed train,
    O doubt it not! through Him they pray:

Like one that runs and never faints,
 Borne up by strength beyond his own,
That fervent charity of Saints
 With eagle flight surrounds the throne.

Strong love, that stirs the bowers of rest!
 New partners of their joy they crave;
" Bring all, O Father, to Thy breast,
 Yon struggling Church uphold and save."
From Mary Mother in her bliss
 To Saints whose white is newly worn,
All strive with eager cry like this
 To speed Thy work, O Virgin-born!

Ah, dearest Lord—ah, sacred Heart!
 Thine, first and last, the work must be;
None else therein can claim a part,
 For none has borne our sin save Thee.

Alas, that Christian hearts should e'er
    Keep Christ at distance in their need,
Or all His servants' love compare
    With that which made the Five Wounds bleed !

Therefore to Thee our prayer goes up,
    Therefore to Thee our heart is given :
For Thou alone didst drink the cup,
    And Thou art man's High Priest in heaven :
In fellowship with friends above
    O make us tread their upward way,
Till simply, solely through Thy love,
    We stand beside them on that Day !

The Sympathies of Christ.

"ONE Person in two Natures,—God and
   Man;"
On this high rock Thy Church's feet are set;
So at Chalcedon her confession ran,
   And so she owns Thee yet.

But oft the mind, in this our pilgrim state,
   Truth in two aspects can but dimly see;
And in our weakness oft we separate
   What thus are joined in Thee.

So, knowing all God's worship to be Thine,
    We strain our souls to praise Thee, Light of Light!
But Thou art not less human than Divine,
    Thy Manhood claims its right.

We say, "He searcheth all things—through and
    through
Scans what arose from nothing at His call;
Therefore He knows our sorrows." True, O true!
    But, Brother! is that all?

Thou took'st on Thee this flesh and soul of ours;
    And they, by that assumption glorified,
And now enriched with yet sublimer powers,
    For ever Thine abide.

And therefore, O most merciful High Priest!
    Thy human Heart is strong to sympathize
At once with all Thy chiefest and Thy least;
    All meet those pitying eyes.

All claim alike the fulness of Thy care,
    That rests on all as each, on each as all ;
The world-wide Church—a little one at prayer—
    A village bier and pall ;

Watchers that strive for hope when hope is none ;
    Spirits worn out with lonely grief or pain ;
Each tearful mother pleading for the son
    She ne'er may greet again ;

The faithful met to share the Sacrifice ;
    Pastors in toil, and minds oppressed with doubt ;
Wanderers that groan, " I will, I will arise,
    He will not cast me out ;"

All these, and every soul Thy Blood has bought,
    May find in Thee a perfect human Friend ;
To each the vastness of Thy human thought
    Doth full attention bend.

And as Thy Flesh is ne'er bestowed in part,
So comes entirely, simply, as a whole,
This real Presence of Thy mind and heart
To each believing soul.

So let us welcome this surpassing grace,
This wondrous fruit of Incarnation's tree ;
Spring forth to meet Thy brotherly embrace,
And yield our hearts to Thee.

"Ubi Charitas et Amor*."

WHERE is Love's abode,
There we find our God.
One and all for love of Christ assembling,
Let us find in Christ our joyous cheer;
Serve the living God with love and trembling,
To our brethren cleave with hearts sincere.
Where is Love's abode,
There we find our God.

* From the Roman office for washing the feet on Maundy Thursday.

So when thus as brothers we are meeting,
    Take we heed that nought our souls divide ;
Sounds of strife and malice far be fleeting,
    So shall Christ our God with us abide.
        Where is Love's abode,
        There we find our God.

So 'mid all Thy Saints with exultation,
    Christ our God, Thy Face may we behold ;
O the pure joy, passing estimation,
    Through the life that endless years unfold !
        Where is Love's abode,
        There we find our God.

Hymn for the Close of a Service.

AND now the wants are told, that brought
    Thy children to Thy knee;
Here lingering still, we ask for nought,
    But simply worship Thee.

The hope of Heaven's eternal days
    Absorbs not all the heart,
That gives Thee glory, love, and praise,
    For being what Thou art.

For Thou art God, the One, the same,
    O'er all things high and bright;
And round us, when we speak Thy Name,
    There spreads a heaven of light.

O wondrous peace, in thought to dwell
    On excellence Divine;
To know that nought in man can tell
    How fair Thy beauties shine!

O Thou, above all blessing blest,
    O'er thanks exalted far,
Thy very greatness is a rest
    To weaklings as we are;

For when we feel the praise of Thee
    A task beyond our powers,
We say—"A perfect God is He,
    And He is fully ours."

Hymn before a Journey.*

N ways of peace and gladness
   The Lord our footsteps guide,
And His benignant Angel
   Be present at our side,
To bring us, safe and thankful,
   Where we would fain abide.

Send forth, O God, Thy blessing
   From Thy most holy place;
Be Thou a tower of refuge
   From the adversary's face,
And let our souls go onward
   In thy sweet paths of grace.

---

* Partly from the "Itinerarium" of the Breviary.

O be our ways directed
    Thy righteous laws to keep ;
Make straight the crooked places,
    And smooth the pathway steep ;
And bid Thine Angels guard us
    With eyes that never sleep.

Come, Thou that led'st our father
    From Ur of the Chaldee ;
Who mad'st Thy pilgrim nation
    Pass dryshod through the sea ;
Whose bright star led the Sages
    To find and worship Thee.

Come, Saviour, as Thou camest
    On that first Easter Day,
What time the two disciples
    To Emmaus took their way ;
Make *our* heart burn within us,
    And ever near us stay.

HYMN BEFORE A JOURNEY.

O come, Divine Companion
  Along life's changeful road;
And prosper all our journey
  To Thy dear Saints' abode,
The one continuing City,
  The Holy Mount of God.

Hymn for Passion-tide.

"UPON the Cross He died,
    He died that we might live :"
The acts that have this faith denied,
    O injured Lord! forgive.

Once more to Thee we turn,
    Who livest, and wast dead;
But yet our thoughts can scarce discern
    Thy wounded hands outspread.

When faith prevailed o'er sight,
    In sterner, simpler days,
Thy Passion cast a solemn light
    On hourly works and ways.

To heart and mind it spoke,
  With tears it filled the eye;
Full oft the spell of sin it broke,
  And brought the far-off nigh.

It bade them number o'er
  The scars themselves had made;
They heard a voice—"All this I bore,
  And am I thus repaid?"

But now some earthly chill
  Can soon our prayers subdue;
Can bring to nought our better will,
  And hide the Cross from view.

We look, we cry to Thee;
  O grant us, of Thy grace,
The foulness of our sin to see,
  The sweetness of Thy face.

HYMN FOR PASSION-TIDE.

As divers minds are bent,
   Thy varied sufferings show,
The pangs Thy Body underwent,
   Thy Soul's mysterious woe.

Unveil whate'er may best
   To Thee our spirits draw,
And fill again the world-worn breast
   With contrite, thankful awe.

True Saviour! by Thy Cross,
   And by Thy throne above,
O save us from that sorest loss,
   The loss of faith and love.

Hymn for Michaelmas.

THOU in whom our very manhood
    Paused not on its upward way,
Till it sat where mightiest Angels
    Must adore it and obey,
'Tis with holy pride we bless Thee
    On Thy glorious Michael's day.

Chiefest he of heavenly Princes,
    Patron of Thy chosen race,
He that drove the ancient rebels
    Down to their appointed place,

HYMN FOR MICHAELMAS.

Calls himself the fellow-servant
Of the least that share Thy grace.

Near him shineth one whose glory
  Smote with dread Thy favoured seer;
He that thrice *, with words benignant,
  Lifted off the load of fear;
He that first proclaimed Thy Gospel,
  When he hailed Thy Mother dear.

If no more that radiant presence
  In Thy servants' path is found,
Yet we lean on Thy sure promise,
  Asking not for sight or sound;
Thou, unseen, art watching o'er us,
  And Thy hosts encamp around.

* Dan. x. 19; St. Luke i. 13. 30.

HYMN FOR MICHAELMAS.

So, if once on young Tobias
    Raphael spent a comrade's cares,
Now yet more our several Guardians
    Haste to serve salvation's heirs;
'Tis our part in Thee, O Jesus!
    Wins us all this love of theirs.

Mindful, then, of all good Angels
    In Thy service nobly free,
Let us faintly join their chorus,
    While our festal prayer shall be,—
More and more with them unite us
    In adoring love to Thee.

Grant us, Lord, their zeal for goodness,
    And their loathing hate of ill;
Let their loyal promptness teach us
    How to do the Father's will,

With a keen and steadfast ardour
Each commandment to fulfil.

But we are not, Lord, high-minded;
Well we know how oft we fall;
O let Thy converting Spirit
　　Straight the wandering sheep recall,
Kindling pure Angelic gladness
　　Through the bright celestial hall.

Let Thy grace yet more restrain us,
　　Lest anew from Thee we roam;
And when at Thine awful bidding
　　Our predestined change shall come,
Grant us peace, and give Thine Angels
　　Charge to bear our spirits home.

Let them watch our happy mansions,
 Where the foe can stretch no rod * ;
Till the Judgment's thrilling prelude
 Pierces through the burial sod,
And the great Archangel calls us
 In our flesh to meet our God.

* Psalm cxxv. 3.

Hymn for a Martyr's Day.

SAVIOUR, while we dwell securely
　In this quiet resting-place,
And Thine unpolluted altars
　Ne'er behold a threatening face,
Let us think of all Thy brave ones,
　More than conquerors through Thy grace.

Thou didst make the good confession,
　Thou didst bear the witness true,

Which could all the white-robed Army
  With supernal force endue,
And in their majestic patience
  Somewhat of Thy Cross renew.

Thou wast standing up in glory
  Not for Stephen's sake alone,
But for all—for him whose triumph,
  Save for Thee, were still unknown;
Antipas, Thy faithful Martyr,
  Slain where Satan fixed his throne.

Through the stern campaign we mark Thee,
  Cheering, strengthening, crowning all;
Present when the Cedron valley
  Saw Thy righteous kinsman fall;
When the blood-stained Harlot City
  Slew Thy Peter and Thy Paul.

Thine were they whose mystic voices
    'Neath the altar cried, " How long ?"
Thine was he whose glorious answer
    Showed how love could make him strong;
" Eighty years and six I served Him,
    And He never did me wrong."

Yes, though oft the prime of manhood
    Won the wreath that ne'er decays,
And a Laurence and a Vincent
    Wear the true victorious bays,
Yet in weakest things of this world
    Thou didst win Thee fullest praise.

Ah! 'twas like Thee, O my Jesus!
    Richest grace on these to shed;

On the boyish bloom of Pancras,
    On Pothinus' hoary head,
On the softly-nurtured women
    Following where Perpetua led.

Mothers gladly saw their children
    Death for Mary's Son endure;
Home and lands young Cyril yielded
    For the Martyr's birthright sure;
And the once-polluted Afra
    Gained the palm-branch of the pure.

Virgin lips, their Lord confessing,
    Trembled not for steel or flames;
Agnes, Lucy, Faith, Cecilia—
    'Tis a joy to speak their names!
Let the hand forget her cunning
    If the memory slight their claims.

HYMN FOR A MARTYR'S DAY.

Ah! but none, Thou loving Shepherd,
    Were more precious in Thine eyes
Than apostates of the moment
    Who returned to win the prize,
Saying to the Foe, " Rejoice not,
    Though I fell, He makes me rise."

And the secret of their conquest
    Let Thy Kingdom's records tell;
'Twas the old Faith once delivered,
    Scorned so oft, and proved so well;
They adored Thee, God Incarnate,
    They believed in Heaven and Hell.

Oft Thou heard'st them in the tortures
    Gasping, ere the soul went free—

"Jesus, in Thy cause I suffer—
To Thy Name all praises be!
Rather this—O grant me patience!
Than eternal loss of Thee."

Rather this? O rather all things!
God our Saviour, keep us Thine;
In this age's bloodless conflict
 Let us ne'er that Faith resign;
So at length Thy voice shall own us,
 "These were true to Me and Mine."

An Intercession.

THOU in whose all-pitying eyes
Each pardoned soul is one more prize,
Thy mercy makes it sweet indeed
For cherished friends to intercede.

But since our love would ne'er abound
If pent in too familiar ground,
In thoughtful moments of the day
For those we know not let us pray.

For all whose faces ne'er we see—
But chiefly those, well known to Thee,
Whose perilled, sickly, struggling soul
Cries out for God to make it whole.

Those most of all, for love's dear sake,
Whose need is all the cry they make,
Whose very depth of ill is this,
Their vanished graces ne'er to miss.

Have mercy, Christ! on hearts grown cold,
On sheep that long have left Thy fold;
On souls once full of eyes within,
Now blinded through deceits of sin.

On those, Thine own in earlier youth,
Now coldly asking, "What is truth?"
Who spurn the way their fathers trod,
Forego their faith, and lose their God.

On tempted souls,—O Saviour, think
Of those who touch the awful brink,
And unrepentant, unforgiven,
This very night may forfeit Heaven.

Send help to all whom ease or toil,
Whom care or wealth, would taint or spoil;
To those no less, in pain that lie,
Tempted to curse their God and die.

In garrets foul, in cellars dark,
There are on whom is set Thy mark;
Thou that wast laid in oxen's stall,
O ne'er let misery work their fall.

Once more, for those who never heard
The still small voice of Thy dear Word,
Who in Thy land as heathens roam,
O Christ, we pray Thee,—fetch them home.

Acts of Prayer.

HERE'ER thy knees are bent, 'tis awful ground,
God's throne before thee, and His hosts around:
But turn to Him in whom two natures meet,
His grace divine, His human love entreat:
To God thy Father tell thy guilt and shame,
And pardon crave in God thy Brother's name:
And more than pardon—more He fain would give;
Ask all thou need'st, a worthier life to live:

Nor ask for self alone; He bids thee dare
All, whom thy love can reach, enfold in prayer :
More warmly then thy gratitude shall glow,
In praising Him that makes thy cup o'erflow :
Whose sweetness bids thee trustfully commend
Whate'er thou hast and art to thine eternal Friend.

Temptation.

THOU that lov'st us dearer far
    Than our truest self we love,
Canst re-make whate'er we mar,
    Canst our clinging stains remove,
Canst enrich the barren heart
    With a boon of gracious tears,
And restore, in whole or part,
    E'en the locust-eaten years:

Thou that when we scarce can tell
    If we love Thee, ay or no,—
When, as from some deepest well,
    Fresh temptations ever flow,

When our souls, 'mid strife intense,
    Wage a poor half-hearted fight,—
Still canst be our strong defence,
    Out of weakness bring forth might:

Thou to whom our fathers cried,
    Cried and were not brought to shame,—
Save us from yon billowy tide,
    Snatch us from this brightening flame!
By the precious life-drops spilt
    To wash white our loathsome clay,
Let the thoughts that end in guilt
    From our bosoms pass away.

Thou to whom that sire distraught
    Weeping showed his tortured boy,
Scarce believing, still besought,
    Then could scarce believe for joy;

All we have, O wilt Thou take?
Longings deep our sins to rue;
These are Thine—from these awake
Love unfeigned, and penance true.

Penitence.

 GRANT us, Lord, a contrite heart;
With this our inmost wants begin;
Bid all the selfish ease depart
That blunts and chills our sense of sin.

Thou heard'st our fathers grace entreat
As men that cry 'mid wreck or fire;
Their sons the selfsame prayers repeat
With scarce one spark of true desire.

But Thou canst help us, if Thou wilt—
    Canst make us stand the Cross beside,
And teach us there to loathe our guilt,
    Remembering wherefore Jesus died.

Show us that sin is heartless wrong,
    Good Father! to Thy love so vast,
That bears so much, and waits so long,
    To win Thy children home at last.

Grant us to turn, believe, repent;
    Let Thy sweet grace our hardness kill.
And Thy most Holy Sacrament
    Confirm in good our faltering will.

Prayer after Pardon.

WE know Thee who Thou art,
   Lord Jesus, Mary's Son ;
We know the yearnings of Thy heart
   To end Thy work begun.

That sacred fount of grace,
   'Mid all the bliss of Heaven,
Has joy whene'er we seek Thy face,
   And kneel to be forgiven.

Brought home from ways perverse,
    At peace Thine arms within,
We pray Thee, shield us from the curse
    Of falling back to sin.

We dare not ask to live
    Henceforth from trials free;
But oh! when next they tempt us, give
    More strength to cling to Thee.

We know Thee who Thou art,
    Our own redeeming Lord;
Be Thou by will, and mind, and heart,
    Accepted, loved, adored.

Tribulation and Wealth.

"SUFFERING is learning;" so of old 'twas
    writ*;
And well the pensive minds of Hellas knew
That insolence was oft to grandeur knit,
    And out of power a soul's corruption grew.

Therefore they marvelled at Timoleon's life,
    Bright with success, but self-renouncing still †

---

* Herod. i. 207.   † Grote, Hist. Gr. vii. 601.

Or hers, of kings the daughter, sister, wife,
    Whose heart was ne'er elate with blind self-will*.

The phrase might seem an echo of the Book
    That tells how men, 'mid life's delicious flow,
Their strength or wisdom for their fortress took,
    And were in pride uplifted,—for their woe.

And be the warning precious, whensoe'er
    Soft ease would fan us with her fragrant wings,
And we, too prosperous, in the sunshine fair
    Forget God's presence, and the Four Last Things.

But dare we deem that only in success
    Our life's probation or our danger lies;
That pain, by law of nature, needs must bless,
    And sorrow fix our treasure in the skies?

* Thuc. vi. 59.

Too well we know what fierce unchanging spite
With versatile resource pursues its prey ;
Whose arrows find us when our path is bright,
And pierce us in the dark and cloudy day.

Why else do sinners, for each stroke or loss
More prone to trespass, fill the sacred theme,
Wretches who hang rebellious on a cross,
Who gnaw their tongues for anguish, and blaspheme *?

For pain can harden, grief can isolate,
And chill, too oft, the love that sprang from joy ;
A sudden shock the faith of years abate,
And death's last agonies the soul destroy.

And where, O Christ, is safety? Where indeed,
But in the grace which taught Thy glorious Paul

* Rev. xvi. 10, 11.

How to abound, and how to suffer need,
    To face all changes, and be Thine through all?

To Thee who canst not change, our saving Health,
    Shall this deep prayer by steadfast faith be poured,—
In time of tribulation and of wealth,
    Be near, to save us from ourselves, O Lord.

Patience.

"IN patience make your souls your own*;"
When darksome days were near,
This rule He gave, to guard His flock
From restlessness and fear.

Yet, Lord, from other lips than Thine
The words might seem to speak
Of Heathen calmness, self-upheld
And scorning to be weak;

* St. Luke xxi. 19, κτήσασθε.

The philosophic height of soul,
    That counteth nothing great *,
And in the face of shock or storm
    Relies on power innate.

But all the goodliness of pride
    Thou bidd'st Thine own abjure,
And find in nothingness confessed
    The strength that standeth sure.

Yes; we are nothing—Thou art all!
    That creed, implanted deep,
Shall nerve us, in the evil day
    A good heart still to keep.

If tidings of a wide distress
    Ring like a funeral sound,
With anguish thickening o'er the earth
    And terrors all around;

---

* Arist. Eth. iv. 3.

What joy, to set the Name of Christ
    Between our souls and harm,
And cast the weight of all our care
    On Thy sufficing arm!

What peace, to welcome all Thy will,
    Bid faithless fears depart,
And sanctify the Lord our God
    Within the trustful heart!

So, as of old Thy Spirit's force
    A shrinking prophet steeled *,
To grace in its transforming might
    Shall nature's weakness yield.

For this is man's true dignity,
    To lean on God above;
The kingly power of self-control
    Comes with the gift of love †.

---

* Jer. i. 18.   † 2 Tim. i. 7.

This is the patience born of faith,
That sets the whole man free,
And makes our souls our own in truth,
By offering them to Thee.

Thankfulness.

'TIS not for nothing, Lord, we read
 How, in the Church's golden prime,
The readiest for Thy cause to bleed,
 The men in thought and act sublime,
Whose names beam out like stars in heaven,
 Whose memory all Thy liegemen bless,
Were those to whom Thy love had given
 The boon of life-long thankfulness.

Full well they knew, 'twas meet and right
    To mingle constant praise with prayer,
To render thanks with all their might,
    For all things, always, every where;
So Cyprian with thanksgiving glowed,
    Soon as he heard the doom of death;
And " Praise to God for all things" flowed
    From Chrysostom's departing breath.

But far and wide the grace was cast,
    The seed of love was broadly sown;
By " Deo gratias," as they passed,
    The faithful folk were surest known;
That watchword for the daily strife
    Might well their tongues and thoughts employ,
Who made the Church transform their life,
    And the great Offering crown their joy.

Let their example teach us, Lord,
  One secret of the life divine ;
How in the thankful breast are stored
  Forces that make the whole man Thine.
Who bids his heart go forth in love
  To Thee that far exceed'st it still,
Sets all within him free to move
  In concert with Thine own dear will.

Ah ! well may lives be poor and base,
  When hearts to Thee are hard and cold ;
O grant, in love, that quickening grace,
  Which yet Thy justice might withhold.
Thou that didst turn the flinty rock
  At once into a springing well,
Our closed affection canst unlock,
  And make our lips Thy mercies tell.

So grant us, first, a worthier sense
    Of gifts that form our special share,
Each gracious call and influence,
    Each friend raised up, each answered prayer ;
Then make us wing a broader flight,
    Help us to bless Thee while we scan
The length, and breadth, and depth, and height
    Of Thy redeeming work for man.

But while we long, as long we must,
    More gladness in Thy praise to know,
Preserve us, lest we put our trust
    In keen emotion's fitful glow ;
Let every hymn that thrills the breast
    A duteous habit serve to feed ;
So thankful words shall please Thee best,
    When bearing fruit in life and deed.

A Perfect Heart.

OF all the precious gifts, O Lord,
    Thy mercy can impart,
Whate'er Thou willest to withhold,
    O grant a perfect heart *.

Behold us, how we feebly float
    Through many a changing mood :
How oft one flash of thought annuls
    Our firmest choice of good.

* 1 Chron. xxviii. 9, &c.

We sin, repent, and fondly think
    Our hill is now made strong;
Our state of grace, restored, abides—
    Thou knowest, Lord, how long!

Alas, for prayer-made purposes
    That live not half the day—
For goodness like the morning cloud,
    Like dews that pass away!

Alas, this paltry doubleness
    Puts all our life to shame,
And brands on us, baptized for Truth,
    The self-deceiver's name.

Thou knowest all; but, gracious Lord,
    We know Thou didst intend
That we should hold the one true course
    To Thee, our one true End.

O take our incoherent wills,
  And set them straight with Thine!
Our broken threads of moral life
  In one strong whole combine;

Make us each day more fixed in love,
  To Thee more simply given,
Till Perseverance lands us safe
  In Thine unchanging Heaven.

Zeal.

WHEREFORE ask if Heaven's true pilgrims
   Found less hindrance on their way
In the old rough-handed ages
   Than in our fair modern day?
God keeps watch o'er all probations,
   Helping those that strive and pray.

Ah! but now His pitying Angels
   See full many a fall begin

When this age's worldly softness
    Penetrates the soul within,
Till it looks with half-allowance
    On the ghastly face of sin.

For all facts must have their welcome,
    All opinions claim their right;
And the calm impartial blandness
    So befools our moral sight,
That we scarcely dare to whisper,
    "This is darkness, that is light."

"Ye that love the Lord, hate evil!"
    O let this forgotten lore
Send the fire of just discernment
    Burning through our souls once more;
Make us humbly, bravely zealous
    For the God our lips adore.

Save us, Lord, from base contentment
When Thine honour lacks its due ;
In our chilled and languid spirits
Wake the manful faith anew,
That the vile is not the precious,
And the false is not the true.

Hiding from God.

ITHER from Eden-gates—a long, long
    road!
Yet whoso looks around, too clearly sees
Marks of the twain that hid themselves from God
    Behind the garden trees.

The age denies Him not, but blindly strives
    To thrust His active presence far away,
Back from the scene of daily thoughts and lives
    To some dim elder day.

Little it costs to call Him primal Cause;
  More to confess that, since He reigneth still,
The sequences men deem eternal laws
  Obey His sovereign will;

Yet more, to own His full imperial right
  O'er all the souls and intellects He gave;
And from that claim perpetual, infinite,
  No freedom e'er to crave.

So men, by some dark impulse, break the cord
  That bound their sires to worship and to faith;
They will not know the terrors of the Lord,
  Nor bow to all He saith

Of sin and judgment; no! they cannot brook
  What seems a mystic saying, or a stern;
And from His Church interpreting His Book
  They will not stoop to learn.

And so for solid faith they substitute
A mass of fluid thoughts, but half believed;
And plant the flowers of love, without the root
Of sacred facts received,

Of doctrines strong to heal, amend, uplift;
And finding thus no virtue in a Creed,
They welcome not the all-surpassing gift
Of God made Flesh indeed.

And they whose worldly peace would feel a sting
If the Most High were thought to come so near,
May well ignore His Sacraments, that bring
All Heaven around us here.

So cries the world to Heaven, " Depart from us!"
And shall we with the world our portion choose?
Not thus, all-gracious Lord, O never thus
May we our bliss refuse!

No—let us open wide our spirit's door
    To all that speaks and witnesses of Thee ;
And hasten to the Light, that more and more
    Our lives may lightened be.

O loving Presence ! beam through mind and heart
    Possess us wholly ; come, in fulness come ;
Nor e'er hereafter say, " Let Us depart,"
    But, " This shall be My home."

The Corner Stone, a Stumbling Stone.

ONE mystery of the inner life
   We tremble while we scan ;
God sendeth days with good most rife,
   Most perilous to man.

When sacred truth is fullest taught,
   And grace flows far and wide,
They seem most rudely set at nought,
   Most thanklessly defied.

THE CORNER STONE,

Can hardened hardness be the effect
    Of more outspoken love?
Can He, the Corner Stone Elect,
    A stone of stumbling prove?

Yea, so He willed, who fashioned thus
    The gift of choice we share;
For when He deigns to visit us,
    He lays our spirit bare.

His presence, like a potent test,
    Appealing to our will,
Intensifies within the breast
    Our force of good or ill.

Its voice the wise have understood;
    They cry, "Thy servants hear;"
While some shrink farther from their good,
    Because it comes so near.

A STUMBLING STONE.

A dread rehearsal of the Doom
    Thus holds its gradual sway,
And men far distant from the tomb
    Are judged from day to day;

As each makes answer to the voice,
    In severed ranks they stand;
On each, for every godless choice,
    Is marked a deeper brand.

O set for rising and for fall,
    This tells us why of yore
Thou wouldst not manifest to all
    What loving hearts adore:

So now, whene'er, with wondering grief,
    Thy truth divine we see
Awakening fiercer unbelief
    Where joyous faith should be;

Let no impatience of Thy wrong
Keep back our pitying prayers,
That those for whom Thou tarriest long
May find our Jesus—theirs.

St. Martin's Vision.

AN aged saint was kneeling, rapt in prayer
    'Twas he that more abundantly than all
Had toiled, to chase the idols from their lair
    In forest glades of Gaul.

Ere yet the Font he knew, a soldier lad,
    At Amiens gate, when winter's face was grim,
With half his cloak a shivering wretch he clad,
    So clothing Christ in him.

That loving deed, by Love thus owned and blest,
    Became the sunrise of the bright career
That made, through all God's Churches in the West,
    The name of Martin dear.

Wondrous in works; 'mid furious Heathen brave;
    His teaching with the Name of Jesus rife;
Deep pity in his heart, that yearned to save
    A doomed heresiarch's life.

And he was kneeling, praying through the night,
    When 'mid a splendour as from heaven sent down
A form stood o'er him, beautiful and bright,
    With gorgeous robes and crown.

A sweet voice thrilled him, while his face he raised;
    " Has Martin, then, to own his Lord forgot?
Adore me, O my servant!" Martin gazed,
    Uprose, and worshipped not,

But sternly spake, "His token never fails ;
Against deceivers this be my defence :
Show me in hands and feet the print of nails :—
Thou canst not—Get thee hence !"

O Christ, the same through ages and to-day,
In whose dear form those awful marks endure,
Do not like trials oft our faith assay
With many a dazzling lure ?

Learning and fancy, thought in ample reach *,
And wealth of glowing words, our homage claim :
They haunt our ears with gentle, solemn speech,
And greet us in Thy Name.

Grant us to try them, Lord, by Martin's test ;
And if on this exuberance of mind

---

* See a well-known passage at the end of "The Church of the Fathers."

We see Thy saving Passion's mark imprest,
   To welcome all we find :

If not—the lying spirit to discern,
   Nor follow, to our endless shame and loss,
The teachers who would make our hearts unlearn
   The doctrine of Thy Cross.

Secular Opinion.

YE say, "The chiefs of worldly thought
　　Our motives and our acts misread,
And scan through some deforming mist
　　The beauteous Cause for which we plead.

"Our loyal zeal for Faith they call
　　The instinct of a priestly caste,
A love of dull dogmatic form,
　　A helpless yearning o'er the past.

"They wave us off, they talk us down,
　With subtle sneer and clamour loud ;
At every turn our soul is filled
　With all the scorn of all the proud."

Be patient, friends; look up to Heaven,
　And in the appointed future trust ;
Nor fret if censors do you wrong,
　Who cannot, if they would, be just.

A veil before their sight is spread ;
　The whole grand case they cannot see ;
No marvel if in Babel's ears
　Your Creed an idle tale should be.

They know not that the Faith is true,
　That all high Powers are on your side ;
God's Kingdom and its wondrous work
　Are by their shallowness denied.

SECULAR OPINION.

'Tis lack of sense for greatest things
    That fosters this complacent scorn,
And makes the World in every age
    Against the Church lift up her horn.

Dear friends, accept this little cross,
    And let man's judgment have its way;
And when contemned or slandered most,
    Be patient—think of Christ—and pray:

"Lord, give us brave and cheerful faith,
    To do Thy work and wait Thine hour,
And know, whate'er Opinion's force,
    Thine is the kingdom and the power."

The Greatness of Common Life.

FULL oft in dull unbroken flow
　　The river of our life steals on ;
And thoughts that once could make it glow
　　Are all too willingly foregone.

Some light it takes from Heaven—and yet
　　The round of small prosaic cares
Wins, day by day, more power to set
　　A gulf between us and our prayers.

Our inner self, impoverished thus,
 Becomes a thrall of trivial things;
And O what grand designs for us
 Our paltriness to failure brings!

And still we tread on wondrous ground,
 And need but grace to hear and see
What splendours gird our spirits round,
 What voices call us, Lord, to Thee!

Each least eventful hour is fraught
 With helps and harms no tongue can tell;
Nor leaves us till our souls are brought
 Nearer, one step, to Heaven or Hell.

All day the realms of Love and Hate,
 Of Life and Death, for us contend;
Though tarrying long and coming late,
 Yet each day nearer draws the end.

Think we on both those kingdoms dread;
Nor list the lion roaring nigh,
Without a gaze on hands outspread,
That ceaseless plead for us on high.

Thou Christ enthroned! that form of Thine
Can best light up our common days,
Till earthly tameness grows divine,
And homely work shows forth Thy praise.

Hell.

"NOT true—not true ! our souls protest—
 From that fell yoke our minds are free;"
So raves the cry of fierce unrest—
"Eternal Death? It shall not be !

"For ended faults, an endless pain?
All mercies lost in vengeful ire?
Nay, more—God's justice ye profane,
Who say it feeds a quenchless fire.

" Sooner than woe should aye endure,
    Perish the hope of constant bliss !
Nor say, Christ's words have made it sure ;
    They could not mean a doom like this."

They could not mean ? O blinded hearts,
    What means your strife with that high law
That forms us free to take our parts,
    And makes us hold ourselves in awe ?

Go, read the cause of endless death
    In that dire mystery of a will
That holds, beyond the parted breath,
    Its fixed persistent choice of ill.

Ye dare not say, "No choice can last,"
    Or, "God must needs our freedom quell;"
Then learn, 'tis no mere vanished past
    That calls for penal throes in Hell.

No ! 'tis the soul whose will intense
Survives Probation's measured day,
And, bidding goodness still " Go hence,"
Finds answer, " Take thine own dark way."

Heed this, O man, ere grace be spent ;
To fall from God and scorn to rise,
To sink in woes and ne'er repent,
This makes the death that never dies.

Antichrist.

YES, he will come ; God knoweth when or
    where ;—
But we may see, perchance,
Around us tokens, neither dim nor rare,
    That herald his advance :—
Lord Jesus, root Thy love our hearts within,
Our safeguard when we name the Man of Sin.

Whene'er we look beyond the holiest ground,
    What signs unblest we see !

Such hate of zeal, such earthliness profound,
    Such lack of godly fear,
Such wrath provoked by Doctrine's very name,
Such fixed rejection of Thy Kingdom's claim!

Content with nature, thousands cast out grace
    From their Pelagian creed;
No marvel, then, they give a Church no place
    Whereof they feel no need.
So, when she stands across their state-craft's way,
"No king but Cæsar," sums up all they say.

To scorn her priests, her Sacraments disown,
    Seems but a light thing now;
Men call their conscience,—free, supreme, alone,—
    The Word to which they bow;
And fast outgrow the credence of their youth,
That Christ is God, and all His words are truth.

These are the shadows, gathering darker gloom
    Ere yet the storm breaks out ;
Ere Europe sees a modern Heathendom,
    With wild blaspheming rout,
Break every bond, and cast off every cord
That links the Christian races to their Lord.

And daily bolder grows their downward course
    Who turn from Christ away,
To worship human genius, grandeur, force,—
    Whose hopes await the day
When,—Creed and prayer 'neath feet of Progress trod,—
Earth shall re-echo—" Man alone is God."

Ah! then shall he that leads that cry accurst
    'Mid rebels wear the crown ;
Of worldly heroes proudest, last, and worst,
    Shall see the world bow down,

ANTICHRIST.

Its sin shall concentrate, its power shall wield,
And face the Church as Antichrist revealed.

Apostates' type and chief, and idol too,
    That lawless one * shall tower
Enthroned in temples reared for worship true,
    And have his destined hour
To speak great words against the Lord on high,
And strive to make His saints His Name deny.

Sternest of trials! who shall come forth bright?
    They, only they, that cling,
As with both hands, with heart and soul and might,
    To their Incarnate King :—
Lord, help us now to prize what then shall be
Their one support—the Faith that lives on Thee.

---

* 2 Thess. ii. 8, ὁ ἄνομος. See Archbishop Trench's Five Sermons in 1856, p. 19.

The Atonement.

FATHER in Heaven! when on the Cross we see
Our Substitute who makes amends to Thee,
On whom the burden of our guilt is laid,
In whom Thy truth and mercy shine displayed,
Who into deepest harmonies can draw
Thy sweet compassion and Thy righteous law,
His stripes our health, His bondage our release,
His pain the chastisement that wins our peace;
Who o'er our frailty can His mantle spread,
And make a perfect answer in our stead;
Our Victim, Pontiff, Ransomer, and thus,
In plenitude of meaning, slain *for us;*

THE ATONEMENT.

Forthwith objectors, not of scornful mood,
But jealous for the truth that Thou art good,
Yet all too prompt within themselves to find
A measure of the Eternal will and mind,
With earnest voice the Church's faith reprove,
Saying,—we wrong Thy justice, or Thy love.

Thy love? the soul may answer, "Could there be
Kindness like this, which gives its best for me?
So of God's love I gain a fuller sense,
Than if it triumphed at His law's expense."

Thy justice? Lo, the self-made Sacrifice!
Of pure, benign free will He bleeds and dies;
He that, as second Adam of our race,
By right supreme could stand in all men's place;
And add this grander truth, which, most of all,
Our censors need to ponder or recall,

Of Adam's sons who this life's path have trod,
The Crucified alone was truly God.

Believe but this,—the cause of Faith is won ;
The Father's dealings with the Eternal Son,
Their plan of rescue for our fallen dust,
Above all thought must tower, Divinely just.

Believe but this,—then tax us, friends, no more
With deeming God reluctant to give o'er
His wrathful purpose, till the pleading force
Of Jesu's Blood prevailed to change His course.
No! one in essence, one in majesty,
Father and Son must one in counsel be ;
Not readier this to judge, or that to bless ;
In each all love, in each all holiness ;
The Father's pitying care the Cross ordained,
His own high law of right the Son sustained.

Believe but this,—in awful light shall glow
The healing virtues of that wondrous woe;
What marvel, when the Lord our God most high,
Clothed in our flesh, was lifted up to die,
If then His Godhead to His Manhood gave
Merit and force a thousand worlds to save?
If still ye ask, what reasoning can explain
How Substitution can be aught but vain,
How one can turn aside another's fate,
The question waits for answer;—let it wait.
But note this only,—'tis a faith ye find
Deep in the fountain-thoughts of all mankind;
If hid from sight its primal essence lies,
Prayer is a mystery kin to Sacrifice;
And if sin-offerings mock the soul indeed,
A dark doubt follows—Who can intercede?

The Priesthood.

ATHER of Lights ! that every day
In threescore years and ten
Dost many a gift to us convey
By hands of brother-men ;

Thus joining heart to heart in love,
And training thus the mind
The source of good in Thee above
By growing faith to find ;

What marvel if in things of grace
  Thy rule be still the same;
If in the Church be found a place
  For agents in Thy Name?

So willed of yore, so willeth yet
  Thy Son, by whom we live,
Through stewards o'er His household set
  The food of souls to give.

Their sacred acts, O Christ, are Thine;
  Unseen, yet understood,
'Tis Thou that mak'st the bread and wine
  Thy Body and Thy Blood.

Each babe that feels the christening hand
  Is folded to Thy breast;
Before Thee kneels each faithful band,
  By Thee absolved and blest.

THE PRIESTHOOD.

These acts are all one stream of power
    That from Thy Manhood flows,
And still in every place and hour
    Thy Passion's fruit bestows.

Lord, grant us in Thy Priests to see
    The boon Thy love hath sent;
No barrier 'tween ourselves and Thee,
    But Thine own instrument;

To prize Thy City's glorious things
    As ne'er we prized before;
And so, borne up on eagle-wings,
    Thyself in all adore.

The Evening Absolution.

ANY the soothing rites that Christ doth
make
Our frequent portion here;
But next to that wherein Himself we take,
One seems exceeding dear;
Although the day be weary or be long,
His Absolution comes at Evensong.

In the world's evening was its Helper sent;
As sunlight wore away

He fed the crowds ; His wondrous Sacrament
  Illumed the close of day ;
And shadows fell, in Joseph's burial-place,
On that white covering of the calm dead Face.

The Easter brightness kissed the open grave ;
  When evening came again,
He to His legates the commandment gave
  To pardon or retain.
And fitly thus, at that sweet vesper hour,
His English priests put forth the absolving power.

Ah ! rather say, He puts it forth, who lives
  A Priest for evermore ;
His organs they ; by them He still forgives,
  Who gave the Keys of yore.
They shower abroad His peace ; He bids it find
Meet habitation in the contrite mind.

THE EVENING ABSOLUTION.

Sweet is the preaching of Thy Word—but *this*,
    Dear Lord, this gift divine
To penitents brings home their very bliss,
    Thy Father's peace and Thine :
Whate'er has cheered the day, through toil or rest,
What cancels all its sin, beyond compare is best.

Ritual.

WHEN to Thy beloved on Patmos,
 Through the open door in Heaven,
Visions of the perfect worship,
 Saviour! by Thy love were given,
Surely *there* was truth and spirit,
 Surely there a pattern shown
How Thy Church should do her service
 When she came before the Throne.

O the censer-bearing Elders,
 Crowned with gold and robed in white!
O the Living Creatures' anthem,
 Never resting day or night!

And the thousand choirs of Angels,
With their voices like the sea,
Singing praise to God the Father,
And, O Victim Lamb, to Thee!

Lord, bring home the glorious lesson
   To their hearts, who strangely deem
That an unmajestic worship
   Doth Thy Majesty beseem;
Show them more of Thy dear Presence,
   Let them, let them come to know
That our King is throned among us,
   And His Church is Heaven below.

Then shall Faith read off the meaning
   Of each stately-ordered rite,
Dull surprise and hard resistance
   Turn to awe and full delight;

RITUAL.

Men shall learn how sacred splendour
Shadows forth the pomps above,
How the glory of our altars *
Is the homage of our love.

'Tis for Thee we bid the frontal
Its embroidered wealth unfold,
'Tis for Thee we deck the reredos
With the colours and the gold;
Thine the floral glow and fragrance,
Thine the vestures' fair array,
Thine the starry lights that glitter
Where Thou dost Thy Light display.

'Tis to Thee the chant is lifted,
'Tis to Thee the heads are bowed;

---

* A phrase of Bishop Sparrow's; "Rationale," p. 46.

Far less deep was Israel's rapture
    When the glory filled the cloud.
O our own true God Incarnate,
    What should Christians' Ritual be
But a voice to utter somewhat
    Of their pride and joy in Thee?

What but this? yet since corruption
    Mars too oft our holiest things,
In the form preserve the spirit;
    Give the worship angel-wings,
Till we gain Thine own high temple,
    Where no tainting breath may come,
And whate'er is good and beauteous
    Finds with Thee a perfect home.

St. Tudno's.

"Go up, my son," the Prophet said,
    "And look toward the sea."
Ah! came that summons, in thy thought,
    O Cymric Saint! to thee?

Here, on this grand and solemn height
    Above the Irish main,
Thou stood'st, intent on earthly loss
    And everlasting gain.

And lower, in a cavern-cell,
    Thou mad'st thy stern abode,
To fill thy soul, in loneliness,
    With the great thought of God.

Seven times a day the Orme's Head rocks
    Re-echoed to thy prayer,
Ascending to the Lofty One
    Through this keen mountain air.

And thou would'st haply muse awhile
    On forms of human power,
When thy fierce nation's kingly strength
    Sat throned on Penmaenmawr.

But oh! what peace would wrap thee round,
    As one whom Angels keep,
Oft as thine eyes, at close of prayer,
    Went roaming o'er the deep.

It lay before thee, dark or bright,
    Its voices filled thine ear,
Symbol of God's vast Providence,
    So gentle, so austere.

Majestic sign of power and life,
    High wrath and gracious calm,
Its due-recurring choral tides
    Responded to thy psalm.

Though strange to us thy life and death,
    Yet English faith shall say,
Thou wast among God's witnesses
    In that wild ancient day.

And still, where thine own mountain church
    Looks calmly o'er the waves,
And, sight of joy! the blessed Cross
    Gleams fair on recent graves,

We'll honour one that walked with God,
And sought no earthly fame;
And blend with thanksgiving to Christ
His faithful Tudno's name.

The "Angelus" at Lucerne.*

ON the last eve of a glad autumn week,
    Waiting for friends' return,
I marked the dying radiance faintly streak
    Thy roofs and towers, Lucerne.

Then o'er the western heights that find a crown
    In stern Pilatus' head,
The glorious Lake, the old historic town,
    Soft shadows grew and spread.

* Reprinted from the "Englishman's Magazine."

And stillness with them came, profound, intense,
  As if yon cloistral shade
Could breathe a strange sepulchral influence
  All nature to pervade.

No sound of common life the silence broke;
  But, with a thrilling toll,
The Minster belfry raised its voice, and spoke
  Straight to the heart and soul;

The summons to the week's last "Angelus!"
  Its wild unearthly chime
Witnessed of Him, the Word made Flesh for us
  In lowliness sublime.

But whence the subtle magic of those bells?
  Not such the notes that ring
From every steeple that at Easter swells
  Our triumph in our King;

For though what bids us think how Gabriel came
    Uplifts us to rejoice,
A depth of sadness, pity, love, and shame
    Spoke in that belfry's voice.

It seemed to make confession unto God,
    It seemed to plead with man
For Him whose love a patient path has trod
    Since first His work began.

Woe for the wills against their Saviour set
    So fiercely then as now!
Woe for the stubborn knees that will not yet
    Before the Incarnate bow;

For ears that cannot brook the strong full tones
    Of our unfaltering Creed;
For hearts whose hardened earthliness disowns
    The Cross and their own need.

Still, throned in heaven, to dupes of unbelief
    He spreads His hands all day;
They scan His claims, give judgment cold and
    brief,
    And fearless turn away.

" A brave, pure soul,—purest of men, perchance,
    In History's ripe award;
Wronged by the legends, born of fond romance,
    That call Him God and Lord."

These walk in pride, by sparks themselves have
    lit,
    Gross darkness soon to be;
While others in a dreamy cloudland sit,
    Half asking, " Art Thou He?"

Once more, O peerless mystery of grace !
    Thy sweet appeal renew;

Light up dark minds; win souls to Thine embrace;
High forts of doubt subdue.

Speak, till the sons of peace, with hearts unseared,
Led by that voice of Thine,
Find Him each day more glorious, more endeared,
Christ Human, Christ Divine.

St. Gervais, Rouen.

ES—'tis a place that will not be forgot;
Our memories keep it sacred. We had
    stood,
That morn, in Normandy's primatial church,
Old Rouen's grand and solemn Notre Dame,
Where Rollo wild and pious Longsword sleep,
And our own Founder fills a nameless grave *.
Shrunk was its ancient pomp; within the choir
A scanty band of Canons knelt, and one
At the High Altar said the Chapter Mass,
With two church-boys in trailing cassocks red
To serve him and respond. And thence we came

* William of Durham died at Rouen, in 1249.

To fair St. Maclou's, where through gorgeous glass
The soft light fell on bowed communicants,
And still a tablet spoke of Mission held,
And vows Baptismal heartily renewed,
When Louis Seize had not been ten years king,
Nor yet the great uprooting storm had burst
On France's throne and altar. Onward thence,
To that high-towering pile of loveliness,
A shrine of beauty rather than of awe,
St. Ouen, in its wealth of lightsome grace
Greeting the autumn sunshine. Calm it stood,
As if no fierce fanatic Huguenots,
Mistaking sacrilege for godly zeal,
Nor, later, those that warred against all faith,
Had e'er profaned it.
     Then a gentle slope
Ascending, soon we reached the simple fane,
Sole relic of St. Gervais' Priory,
Where once to Norman William's dying ear,

ST. GERVAIS, ROUEN.

Pealing across the city, swept the toll
Of deep Cathedral bells, announcing Prime ;
And then, with lifted hands, and blinded prayer
To Mary, as if nearer than her Son,
The hard stern kingly spirit left its corse
To lie three hours neglected on the ground,
Till, for the love of God and Normandy *,
At his own cost a simple knight began
The obsequies, through Ascelin's righteous claim
So hardly brought to close.   Had e'er the Psalm
That warns us, man's estate is vanity,
A fuller comment than the Conqueror's end?

Such scenes before him pass, who musing stands
Beside St. Gervais' walls.   But O the change,
Soon as he gains the little crypt below!
Its age by Roman brick-work manifest,
It still survives, a Basilic complete,

* Ord. Vital. vii. 16.

ST. GERVAIS, ROUEN.

With nave and choir, and apse for holiest place,
And the twin sockets for the chancel-veil,
And the stone altar with its crosses five,
And traces of a seat pontifical,
And arched recesses where for ages lay
The first of Rouen's prelates, and the next,
Till fear of Northmen bore the sacred bones
To safer sheltering. Be the memory blest
Of Mello and Avician! O'er their graves,
Haply, Victricius—he who, one has deemed*,
First sang the great " Quicunque,"—he who bore
The staff at Rouen, while o'er Hippo rose
The light of all the west,—this temple reared.

O precious monument of that good time,
When Martin still was at his Master's work,
And seed well sown by blessed Hilary
Was gladdening Angels by its glorious fruit!

* Harvey on the Three Creeds, ii. 577.

ST. GERVAIS, ROUEN. 137

O famous Church of France! in this thy day
Of loyal strife with Satan's ministers,
Whose courtesies, more odious than their scorn *,
Blaspheme thy Lord and God, both thine and ours,
What best will serve thee? Not the Marian zeal
That finds at Bon Secours its own high place;
That fond perversion of His Mother's name,
Wronging His work, His love, His majesty,
Weakening the weakness of His little ones,
And further yet estranging minds estranged;—
But that pure, manful, thoughtful faith and love,
That grand intensity of Christian force,
That knowledge of their country's deepest need,
Whereby thine ancient heroes, preaching Christ
In His Incarnate fulness, fought and won.

He that revives His work in midst of years
Can give whate'er He wills to us and thee.

* See Dr. Pusey on Daniel, p. 30.

O more and more to Saints of either land
May He fulfil His promise ; "I will pour
My Spirit on thy seed!"
                                    And who, meanwhile,
Holding the faith of Christ, could set his feet
In that historic city, where the past
So mingles with the present, nor take home
The true, true lesson, which we that day read
In her Archbishop's annual pastoral,
Fixed on a pillar of St. Vincent's church?
"Lo, all things change, and all things pass away,
And all things die, but faith, and hope, and love ;
These die not, brethren! O how all around,
All divers turns of life, conspire to show
That prodigality of tenderness
Wherewith our God entreats us—Come to Me!"

The Scillitan Martyrs.

'TWAS in July*, in Claudius' consulate,
At Carthage, when the Court was duly met,
Speratus and his fellows, brethren twain
And sisters three, were cited to attend.

Then Saturninus the Proconsul spake;
"Ye may win pardon from Severus, and
From Antoninus, Emperors both, and Lords,
By turning to our gods with right good will."
Speratus said, "We never wrought a crime,
Nor followed after aught of wickedness,
Nor spake to any man an evil word.

---

* About A. D. 200. The lines are a translation from Ruinart's "Acta Sincera."

'Tis you that did us wrong, while we have still
Been rendering thanks; for He whom we adore
Is the true King and Lord." "High-bred are we,"
Quoth Saturninus, " courteous and refined ;
And by the genius of our lord we swear,
And for his weal make vows—and why not ye ?"
Speratus said, " Lend me a quiet ear,—
Our mystery of meekness thou shalt learn."
" Tell out thy mystery ; I will harm thee not ;
Swear only by the genius of our lord."
"The genius of the Emperor of this world
I know not; but I serve my God in heaven,
Whom no man e'er hath seen, nor e'er can see.
My hands are clean of theft; whate'er I buy,
I pay the Emperor tribute, for I know
He is my lord; but worship give I none
Save to my Lord, the King of kings, and Lord
Of all the nations." The Proconsul said,
" Peace to the tumult of your restless tongues !

Draw near, and to the gods do sacrifice."
"Nay," said Speratus; "evil restlessness
Is that which leads to taking of men's lives,
And slanderous charges."
      Turning to the rest,
Spake the Proconsul; "Do not ye take part
In this man's frantic folly; rather fear
Our sovereign, and his ordinance obey."
Answered Cittinus; "We have none to fear
Save Him that is in heaven, the Lord our God."
Then the Proconsul; "Thrust them down again
Into the dungeon; set them in the stocks
Until the morrow."
     When the morrow came,
On his tribunal the Proconsul sat,
And had them brought before him. There they
  stood;
Then spake he to the women; "Pay regard
Unto our sovereign, and do sacrifice."

Donata said, "We render honour due
To Cæsar, as to Cæsar; to our God
Honour and prayer." Vestina, standing, spake;
" I am a Christian too." Secunda next;
"And I too, I believe in mine own God,
Desiring to be found in Him; thy gods
We will not serve nor worship."

                            Hearing this,
He bade them to be kept apart awhile,
Then called the men, and to Speratus said;
" Dost thou persist in being Christian still?"
"Yea," said Speratus; "yea, I do persist;
And hear ye all,—a Christian man am I."
Then all that with him had been put in ward
Heard his confession, and gave full assent,
Saying, "We too are Christians, e'en as he."
Then the Proconsul; " Have ye then no mind
To take fresh counsel, or to gain reprieve?"
Answered Speratus; " In a righteous strife

THE SCILLITAN MARTYRS.

Reprieve is none. Do even as thou wilt;
Since we for Christ will die rejoicingly."
Spake the Proconsul; "Say what books are those
That ye with reverence read?" "The Gospels
 four,"
He answered, " of our Master Jesus Christ,
And the Epistles of the Apostle Paul,
And every Scripture book inspired of God."
Then the Proconsul spake; "I grant you now
Space of three days, for coming to your mind."
Speratus answered; "Christians are we all,
I and these with me; and we will not swerve
From the true faith of Jesus Christ our Lord.
Do what thou wilt."
                        He saw their stedfast mind,
Their faith unshaken; and he bade his scribe
Write down the doom: "All these" (he named
 them all)
" As Christians self-declared, and to our lord

Refusing to give honour and respect,
I sentence to beheading." Soon as this
Was from the tablet read, Speratus spake,
And his companions with him; " Thanks to God,
Who deigns this day in Heaven to welcome us,
As Martyrs, for confession of His Name."

This said, they led them forth. With one accord
They bent their knees, and when a second time
They had given thanks to Christ, the head of each
Was stricken off.
     'Twas in the month July,
The seventeenth day, that they were consummate
As Christ's true Martyrs; and they plead for us
To Jesus Christ our Lord, to whom be given,
With God the Father and the Holy Ghost,
Honour and glory evermore. Amen.

The Vision of Saturus.*

THIS was my vision. We had suffered all,
Had passed from out the flesh, and had begun
A journey eastward, borne by Angels four,
Albeit with their hands they touched us not.
They bore us, yet we moved not as supine,
But as men do that climb a gentle slope.

* About 202. Translated from Ruinart.

And when set free from earth, we first beheld
A light immense; and to Perpetua then,
For she was by my side, " Behold," I said,
" What the Lord promised; now 'tis ours indeed."
And while the Angels bore us on, we reached
A mighty space, as 'twere of garden ground,
Where rose-trees grew, and every kind of flower.
The trees were like the cypress for their height,
And ceaseless fell their leaves. And there we found
Four other Angels, brighter than the rest,
Who, seeing, did us honour, and exclaimed,
Admiring, to their fellows, " Lo! they come,
They come!" Whereon the four that carried us
Were struck with awe, and set us on our feet;
And so we fared along, a stadium's length,
On a broad way, and met Astaxius,
Jocundus, Saturninus, Martyrs all
In this same persecution, burnt alive,

With Quintus, who himself a Martyr died
While yet in prison; and we asked of them
Where dwelt the rest. But then the Angels spake;
"Come first and enter in, and greet the Lord."

Then came we near a place whereof the walls
Seemed built of light; and at the gateway stood
Four Angels, who on all that entered in
Put garments white. So clad, we entered in,
And saw a light immense, and heard a sound
Of many voices, that unceasingly
Cried "Agios! Agios! Agios!" In the midst
We saw One seated, like a white-haired man,
With snowy hair and youthful countenance,
Whose feet we saw not. On His left and right
Were four-and-twenty elders; at their back
Stood many others. And we entered in
Greatly amazed, and stood before the Throne:
And the four Angels held us up, and then

We kissed Him, and He passed His hand across
Our faces. Then the other elders spake;
"Let us stand up." We stood; the Peace went
 round.
Again they said to us, " Go forth, and play."
Then I ; " Perpetua, now thou hast thy wish."
" Yea, thanks to God," she answered; "in the
 flesh
Right glad I was, but now still gladder here."
So passed we forth. . . . . .
        And standing at the gate,
We came to know by face a multitude
Of brethren and of Martyrs ; and we all
Drank in a fragrance rich beyond all words,
That satisfied all cravings, e'en like food.
Then I awoke rejoicing.

St. Fructuosus.

N the Lord's day the soldiers came to seek
The Bishop Fructuosus *. Now he sat
In his bed-chamber. When the lictor's wand
Smote on the door, he tarried not, but rose
With slippered feet, went forth, and faced the men.

"Come," said they, "thou art summoned to appear,
Thou and thy Deacons." "Let us go," he said;

* Bishop of Tarragona: martyred Jan. 21, 259. Translated from Ruinart.

" But let me put the shoes upon my feet."
" E'en as thou wilt," they answered.

                                  So he passed
Within the prison, joyful and assured
Of the Lord's crown to which he had been called,
And prayed, and did not cease. And with him there
Were brethren that to him did minister,
Praying that he would bear them in his mind.
And one day, in the prison, he baptized
Rogatian, now our brother.

                              Six days passed;
And on the Friday, with his Deacons, he
Was brought to trial.

                            Then Æmilian spake,
The Præses; " Bring ye Fructuosus here,
Augurius, and Eulogius." " They attend."
Then he; " The Emperor's mandate ye have heard."

Answered the Bishop; "Naught of that I know;
I am a Christian." "They have given command
To adore the gods." "The One God I adore,
Who made the heaven and earth, the sea, and all
That therein is." "Thou knowest there be gods?"
"I know not." "Soon thou *shalt* know."
                                        To our Lord
The Bishop looked, and inly 'gan to pray.
Æmilian spake; "Who then are heard, who feared,
Who worshipped, if the gods be not adored,
Nor homage to the Emperor's likeness done?"
Then to Augurius; "Do not thou give heed
To Fructuosus." "I adore," said he,
"The God Almighty." To Eulogius next;
"Dost thou, too, worship Fructuosus?" "No,
But Him whom Fructuosus' self adores."

To Fructuosus then Æmilian said,

"Art thou a Bishop?" "Yea, I am." "Thou
wast."
And straight he doomed them to be burned alive.

Then Fructuosus, with his Deacons twain,
Into the amphitheatre was led,
The people mourning for him : such deep love
Not from the brethren only had he won,
But e'en from Heathen ; such a man he was,
As by the Gentiles' teacher, blessed Paul,
The Holy Ghost had shown he ought to be.
And for this very cause the brethren all,
Who knew to what high glory he was bound,
Felt less of grief than joy. Many there were
That in fraternal kindness offered them
A cup of mingled drink ; but he replied,
" Not yet has come the hour to break the fast."
For it was then the fourth hour of the day ;
And on the Wednesday, in their prison-house,

They in due order had the Station kept.
So on the Friday, calm of heart and glad,
He hasted, that in Christ's own Paradise
(Which He for those that love Him hath prepared),
With Martyrs and with Prophets he might feast
And break his Station.

     When they reached the place,
His Reader, Augustalis, straightway came,
And, weeping, begged that he might loose his shoes.
Answered the blessed Martyr, "Nay, my son;
Let be; myself will loose them; strong am I,
Joyful and well assured of what the Lord
Hath promised." When his shoes were off, there
  came
Our fellow-soldier, of the brethren one,
Felix by name, and clasping his right hand,
Craved of the Bishop to remember him.
Then with a loud voice, so that all might hear,
The holy Bishop answered; "I must needs

Be mindful of the whole Church Catholic,
From East to West outspread."

      And standing there,
Just on the verge of entering to receive
The wreath unfading, rather than the doom,
Watched by the soldiers, by the brethren heard,
The Holy Spirit prompting him at once
And speaking in him, Fructuosus said ;
" Ye will not lack a Pastor ; and the love
And promise of our Lord will never fail,
Here or hereafter. For what now ye see
Seems but a sickness lasting for an hour."

So gave he comfort to the brethren round,
And with his comrades to salvation passed ;
Most worthy, and in very martyrdom
Happy to find the promise true, and feel
The Holy Scriptures' profit. They were like
To Azarias and his fellows twain,

ST. FRUCTUOSUS.

For in them, too, the Presence was discerned
Of the All-holy Trinity; for when
They stood within the fire, the Father gave
His help, the Son was near to comfort them,
The Holy Spirit walked amid the flame.
And when the bands that held their hands were
    burnt,
Mindful of prayer, and of their use and wont,
They bent their knees, rejoicing, well assured
Of Resurrection; and with outstretched arms,
In token of the trophy of the Lord,
They poured out prayers to Him, and ceased not,
Until their three souls all went forth as one.

Theodore of Antioch*.

BEFORE Apollo's altar
In Daphne's sacred wood,
With visage pale and anxious
The crowned Apostate stood;
By slaughtered bulls, and incense,
And many a choral strain,
He craved response from Phœbus,—
For hours he sought in vain.

* See Soc. iii. 18, 19.   Soz. v. 19, 20.

THEODORE OF ANTIOCH.

Like Baal's priests on Carmel,
    For fire-sign struggling hard,
So found he none to answer,
    Nor any to regard ;
Till trembling, as with anguish,
    At length the pontiff said,
" If thou wouldst end his silence,
    First take thou hence the Dead.

" For know, thy brother Gallus
    Erewhile the coffin laid
Of Babylas the Bishop
    Within this holy glade :"
" No marvel," Julian answered,
    That no response might come ;
Go, warn the Galilæans
    To bear the carcase home."

We heard, we rushed from Antioch,
  Our buried Saint we found;
High on a car we raised him,
  With chanters gathering round;
And forth the Psalm went thundering,
  " Confounded be all they
That worship carved images,
  To gods of stone that pray!"

The Tyrant heard, and quivered
  With mingled wrath and fear;
" Haste, bid the Prefect Sallust
  Before our throne appear."
He came, and heard the mandate;
  "Avenge me on that crew!
Let those that scorn the Immortals
  Their pride in torments rue."

A Heathen man was Sallust,
　　Enslaved to Cæsar's will;
Yet loth in Christian Antioch
　　Such bidding to fulfil.
Since vain were prayer and counsel
　　To move that soul accurst,
He stretched his hand for victims,
　　And seized on me, the first.

To that fell Horse of torture
　　Affixed at prime of morn,
I hung till hour of vespers,
　　All mangled, wrenched, and torn;
Yet still had strength for chanting,
　　" Confounded be all they
That worship carved images,
　　To gods of stone that pray!"

Ah! marvel not, Rufinus;
I am but flesh and blood;
My pangs at first were grievous,
But soon beside me stood
A young man, tall and beauteous,—
O friend, believe me now!—
Who wiped with cool soft linen
The sweat from off my brow.

In that sweet Angel-presence
The pain could scarce abide;
He sprinkled water o'er me,
He stirred not from my side,
Till Sallust bade them loose me
Just ere the close of day;
And I could scarce be thankful,
For then *he* passed away.

Unmeet for healing wonders,
  A sinful man was I;
But God may well show tokens
  When kings His Christ defy.
Be Christ Himself my witness,
  That thus He sent me aid,
Who of the doomed Apostate
  That dire example made.

The Battle of Varna.*

ING Ladislas sat with his peers at the
board,
When the peace was made fast with the Moslemah's
Lord;
All welcomed the pledge, "To the first sight of
home!"
All, save Father Julian, the Legate of Rome.

With his stern glooming brows 'midst the banquet
he rose—
"On your compact with Death be confusion and
woes!

* A.D. 1444. See Gibbon, viii. 130. These lines are reprinted from the " Englishman's Magazine."

Who keeps the foul peace, on the Cross he hath
   trod;
Break faith with Mahound, or be faithless to God.

" Your swords might have guarded the Constantines'
   seat,
But ye cast loose the quarry that swooned at your
   feet;
Ho, ye that spare Agag, for Baal that plead,
Trow ye God hath no vengeance, and traitors no
   meed?

"There were days when the Hermit of Amiens
   outspoke,
And chanting, 'God wills it!' all Christendom woke;
O who shall rekindle the light that has fled?
There were days—they are gone! there were men
   —they are dead!

"But ye swore on the Gospels? Our Lady forefend
Her Son's Name should make His worst foeman
   your friend :
'Tis the Pontiff, His Vicar, that cancels your vow,
That speaks by my voice; will ye hesitate *now* ?"

His proud eye flashed round, but no murmur replied,
Till sudden, "God wills it!" King Ladislas cried;
"Thou hast conquered, Lord Legate! next morn,
   by the Rood,
We'll redden yon treaty in Amurath's blood.

"Mount, Knights, for the Cross!" To the saddle
   they sprang;
Through the tents at deep midnight the trumpet-
   call rang;
See the arms, newly donned, in the morning-beam
   glow,
As the tempest of Christendom bursts on the foe!

THE BATTLE OF VARNA.

Cries the Legate, as backward the Moslems recoil,
" They flee, and our household divideth the spoil!"
To the Soldan grey warriors are muttering, " 'Tis o'er!"
But he speaks, calm and solemn—" I've *one* weapon more."

From the folds of his mantle the Treaty he drew,
With a king's written pledge that the peace should be true;
" As we keep faith and troth, brother Soldan, with thee,
So help us our Helper, the Son of Marie."

In the pure face of Heaven he raised it on high,
To plead for revenge on the Nazarene's lie;
Then lifted his voice—to Mohammed for aid
'Twas to Issa Ben Mariam the Infidel prayed.

"Hear, God of the Christians, by Christians defied!
By Thy Name they have sworn—by Thy Name
    they have lied :
If Thou art what they deem Thee, look forth from
    Thy throne,
And do right to my wrongs in avenging Thine own."

Lo the Turks, how they rally, when sorest bestead!
How their "La-illah" peals, and their sabres glow
    red!
Is Michael's own force in each Moslem to-day,
That they turn their pursuers to flight and dismay?

And the Legate rides fast—but he spurreth in vain
Who rides from God's wrath!—see him stretched on
    the plain,
With a doom written deep in those features of woe,
"Who are false for the Truth, have the Truth for
    their foe."

A Tradition of Culloden.

THEY found him on Culloden heath,
    A sight for soldiers' tears;
His beauty all too strong for death,
    His life but twenty years;
They muttered low, "God send him grace!"
    The gory plaid they drew
For corpse-hood o'er the fair, proud face,
    And eyes of lustrous blue.

They bore him past an ancient hall,
    Deep set in vernal trees;
The Lady looks o'er terrace wall,
    The heavy sight she sees;

Her only son, in Urquhart-glen,
    With kinsmen bides afar ;
She will not call him home again,
    Till sinks the blast of war.

Her joy is in that precious life
    Fenced round and kept secure
From gathering clans and deadly strife,
    And dark Drummossie-muir ;
" Far other weird was thine, poor youth ! "
    She bids the bearers wait ;
Her bosom thrills with woman's ruth,
    Her hand unbars the gate.

She looks upon the long bright hair,
    And fast her tears outflow ;
"Some mother's heart, my darling fair,
    Beside thee lieth low !

God's kindness cheer that stricken heart!
   He hath been kind to me;
Else, haply, e'en as now thou art,
   So might my Ronald be."

Her own soft hands the corpse will streek;
   She draws the plaid away :—
Comes ghastly whiteness o'er her cheek,
   Her lips are cold as clay;
Ah! close her arms the dead enfold,
   Her lips to his are pressed;
The mother's heart lies still and cold
   Upon her Ronald's breast.

Louis the Seventeenth.

AS *he* a King of France? He never sat
Wrapt in blue robes, on throne high-
. canopied
And bright with golden lilies; ne'er for him
In long procession from St. Rémi's Church,
Through the old sacred city's crowded streets,
To that sublime Cathedral porch was borne
The oil that blessed the long-lived Monarchy,
In the Ampoule of Clovis. Ne'er for him,
As having "grasped the guidance of the realm,"

Through Notre Dame rang out the choral prayer.
Versailles ne'er called him master; no behest
Of his, from Bed of Justice proudly given
In the Grand Chamber of the Parliament,
Fixed on the rolls his absolute decree.
No private wrath, armed with his manual sign,
Darkened the dark Bastille with new despair.
Nor wars he made, nor peace; no rival Court
His policy discussed, his envoys heard.
No courtier prelate to his lofty stall
Bowed, ere he spoke the message of a King
That ne'er accepteth persons; by his bed,
When hope was o'er, no Almoner appeared,
From jewelled pyx to draw the Host, and breathe
The " Ecce Agnus " in his dying ear,
And say " Inclina " o'er the shrouded corpse,
Ere yet St. Denis' vault should claim its own *.

* See Carlyle, Fr. Rev. i. 28. 31.

LOUIS THE SEVENTEENTH.

He King of France ? that woeful captive boy,
Torn from his mother's arms, and made the prey
Of a coarse ruffian with a tyrant's heart,
Fit for his fiendish task, to brutalize
And slay by inches Louis Capet's son ;
Or freed from those base hands, but left to lie
In sickness, filth, and killing solitude,
Pent in a den with foulest vapours rank,
As if some pest were holding revel there ;
Then, all too late, to gentler guards consigned,
Who could but faintly cheer his last decay,
Teach him that earth had still some kindness left,
And win some fragments of slow mournful speech,
" And yet I ne'er did harm to any one "—
" Ah ! let me see *her* once before I die !"

Yet many owned him King ; all Europe o'er,
Princes or subjects, whoso loathed or feared
The wild Republic, for his rescue prayed.

His uncle, with an exile's parody
Of princely state, assumed the formal style
Of Regent of his kingdom. King he was
To emigrants, in England finding bread ;
To royalists suspected or proscribed,
Gentle or simple, hidden, hunted, caught,
Flung into dungeons, mocked with trial-forms
At Tinville's bar, or bound to Sanson's plank,—
Or living through the Terror, strangely safe ;
To Toulon, when she welcomed England's flag ;
To those high faithful hearts in La Vendée,
That coupled in one joyous battle-cry
His name with God's. Ah! could he but have heard
The shout that startled Dol, when from their knees
Men rose absolved, and rushed upon the foe—
"God save the King! We march to Paradise!"
Or known the simple wish that, victory won,
And France through them to loyal peace restored,
The Seventeenth Louis, of his regal grace,

Would deign but once to visit La Vendée!
Ah! many a King of France might well have given
Whole years of pomp or conquest, but to gain
Place in the prayers and hopes and dying thoughts
Of men like "Anjou's Saint," Cathélineau,
Or Bonchamps, true to mercy e'en in death,
Or such a sweet-souled hero as Lescure!

And History gives their helpless, crownless Liege
His station in the grand old dynasty
That sprang from Hugh of Paris. Past and gone
Is all the splendour of the Fleur-de-lis;
But in the Louvre, where an Emperor's care
Hoards many a relic of old majesties,
A little plaything cannon bears the name
Of the young Seventeenth Louis.
      Let him keep
That title, his by blood, and—better still—
His by a nature which no barbarous wrongs

Could e'er make quite unroyal. Simon once,
(Who saw him kneel upon his wretched bed,
And join his hands as if in act to pray,
Then with demoniac fury fell on him
For " saying Paternosters like a monk,"—
And whom, ere long, the axe of Thermidor
Sent to the judgment of the orphan's God,)
This Simon asked him, " Could the brigands' force
Enthrone thee France's monarch, how wouldst
    thou
Deal with me, Wolf-cub ?" " I would pardon you."

    There spoke the heart of a Most Christian King.
O guiltless victim! dreamed we of a God
In whose decrees were nought unsearchable,
Whose working must be measured, weighed, and
    squared
Precisely with what men call good and just,
How should we look on such a fate as thine ?

But minds that frame such idol-god as this
Know not the Saviour's Cross, the Christian's
    Heaven;
And thou, St. Louis' heir, whose feeble breath,
Just flitting from the poor exhausted form,
Spoke of sweet music and thy mother's voice,
Hast been in Paradise these seventy years *.

        * He died June 8, 1795.

The Odyssey, I. 1—95.*

ING, Muse, the change-tried man who wandered far,
Since o'er Troy town he brought the storm of war;
Saw many a people's burgh, and learned their mind,
And crossed the deep, to many a woe resigned,
Striving his life to save, and home to bear
His comrades; yet not all his love and care
Could save them; by their own self-will undone,
Fools! they devoured the cattle of the Sun,
Who therefore doomed them ne'er their home to see:

* Reprinted from the "Englishman's Magazine."

Of this, beginning where it pleaseth thee,
O Zeus-born Goddess, tell the tale to me.

Now all the chiefs who 'scaped destruction's steep,
At home were safe from battle and the deep;
Save him, for wife and home with longing pained,
Him, whom Calypso in her caves detained,
Fair nymph and goddess, fain her guest to wed.
Yet, when revolving years the season sped
For his home-journey by the Gods decreed,
Not yet from trials was the sufferer freed,
Nor with his loved ones. But the Immortals rued
His lot; save one, whose ceaseless wrath pursued
Godlike Odysseus, till his land he won.
But to the Æthiops was Poseidon gone,
Who dwell at earth's two ends, in west and east,
On hecatomb of sheep and bulls to feast.

There sate he, joyous; while his fellows all
Were gathered in the Olympian Father's hall,
Who of Ægisthus' death himself bethought,
By Agamemnon's heir Orestes wrought;
This he, beginning, to their memory brought.

' " Lo ye! what blame on Gods do mortals throw!
From us, they ween, from us their evils flow;
While they in their own wilfulness create
New sorrows, more than all assigned by fate.
So took Ægisthus, not by fateful doom,
Atreides' wife, and when her lord came home
Slew him, well knowing woes that should betide;
For we had warned him by the Argicide,
' Thou shalt not slay the king, nor court his wife;
Else vengeance shall arise against thy life,
Soon as Orestes shall his country seek
In strength of manhood.' Thus did Hermes speak;

But the good counsel ne'er Ægisthus swayed—
And now, at once, all forfeits he hath paid."

Athene, blue-eyed Goddess, made reply:
"O Father, Cronos-born, of powers most high,
Surely his death was his befitting meed,
And so die all who imitate his deed!
But for Odysseus is my soul opprest,
Woe-worn, and far from all who love him best,
In a lone isle, the centre of the seas,
Where, in her mansion sheltered round by trees,
Abides a Goddess, crafty Atlas' child,
(Atlas, who knows the deep's recesses wild,
And grasps the pillars tall that hold apart
The earth and Heaven); 'tis she that breaks the
    heart
Of her sad captive, fondling him the while
With ceaseless words of blandishment and guile,

To make Odysseus Ithaca forget :
In vain ! on that dear isle his mind is set ;
Could he but see its smoke's ascending wreath,
Hushed were his longings—he would welcome death.
And has thy heart no pity for this pain?
Did he not please thee oft with victims slain
Beside the Argive fleet, on Trojan shore ?
Why then in wrath afflict him evermore?"

To whom the God that drives the stormy cloud :
"O daughter, why are words like these allowed
To pass thy lips ? Bethink thee, could I e'er
Forget the great Odysseus, past compare
Wisest of men, and heedfullest to give
Due sacrifice to those in Heaven that live
For ever ? No—'tis all Poseidon's ire,
The earth-surrounding God, the indignant sire
Of him whom thine Odysseus hath made blind,
Huge Polyphemus, chief of Cyclop kind,

Whom nymph Thoosa bore (the daughter she
Of Phorcys, ruler of the unfruitful sea),
Who met Poseidon in a cavern's grot.
Since then the stern Earth-shaker slays him not,
But keeps him still a wanderer from his home.
But now, that he to Ithaca may come,
'Tis meet we all in council here combine;
So must Poseidon needs his wrath resign,
For vainly, if apart he stands as one,
Against the Immortals will he strive alone."

To him the blue-eyed Goddess made reply:
"O Father, Cronos-born, of powers most high,
If now indeed the blest ones will it so,
That wise Odysseus to his home should go,
To send our envoy, Hermes, it were well
Unto Ogygia's island, straight to tell
The fair-haired nymph our council's firm decree,
That the long-patient chief restored shall be

To Ithaca : and thither I repair,
To kindle force and spirit in his heir;
Who, roused to act, shall to the assembly call
The long-haired Greeks, and bid the suitors all
Pass forth from out his courts, where every day
His fatted sheep and hornèd beeves they slay.
Then will I send him o'er the wave, to learn
Haply some tidings of his sire's return,
At sandy Pylos, and at Sparta's town,
And gain in all men's eyes a fair renown."

LONDON:
GILBERT AND RIVINGTON, PRINTERS,
ST. JOHN'S SQUARE.

A

SELECT LIST OF WORKS

PUBLISHED BY

MESSRS. RIVINGTON,

WATERLOO PLACE, LONDON;

HIGH STREET, OXFORD;

TRINITY STREET, CAMBRIDGE.

Adams's (Rev. W.) The Shadow of the Cross; an Allegory.
A New Edition, elegantly printed in crown 8vo., with Illustrations.
3s. 6d. in extra cloth, gilt edges.

The Shadow of the Cross; an Allegory.

The Distant Hills; an Allegory.

The Old Man's Home; an Allegorical Tale.

The King's Messengers; an Allegory.
These four works are printed uniformly in 18mo., with Engravings,
price 9d. each in paper covers, or 1s. in limp cloth.

A Collected Edition of the Four Allegories, with
Memoir and Portrait of the Author: elegantly printed in crown 8vo.
9s. in cloth, or 14s. in morocco.

An Illustrated Edition of the above Sacred Allegories,
with numerous Engravings on Wood from Original Designs by C. W.
Cope, R.A., J. C. Horsley, A.R.A., Samuel Palmer, Birket Forster,
and George E. Hicks. Small 4to. 21s. in extra cloth, or 36s. in antique
morocco.

Adams's (Rev. W.) The Warnings of the Holy Week; being
a Course of Parochial Lectures for the Week before Easter, and the Easter
Festivals. Fifth Edition. Small 8vo. 4s. 6d.

A

Ainger's (Rev. T.) Practical Sermons. Small 8vo. 6s.

Ainger's (Rev. T.) Last Sermons: with a Memoir of the Author prefixed. Small 8vo. 5s.

A Kempis, Of the Imitation of Christ. A carefully revised translation; elegantly printed by Whittingham, in small 8vo, price 5s. in antique cloth.

Alford's (Dean) Greek Testament; with a critically revised Text: a Digest of Various Readings: Marginal References to Verbal and Idiomatic Usage. Prolegomena: and a copious Critical and Exegetical Commentary in English. In 4 vols. 8vo. 5l. 2s.

Or, separately,

Vol. I.—The Four Gospels. Fifth Edition. 28s.
Vol. II.—Acts to II. Corinthians. Fifth Edition. 24s.
Vol. III.—Galatians to Philemon. Third Edition. 18s.
Vol. IV.—Hebrews to Revelation. Second Edition. 32s.
The Fourth Volume may still be had in Two Parts.

Alford's (Dean) New Testament for English Readers: containing the Authorized Version, with a revised English Text; Marginal References; and a Critical and Explanatory Commentary. In Two large Volumes, 8vo.

Already published,

Vol. I., Part 1, containing the first three Gospels, with a Map of the Journeyings of our Lord, 12s.
Vol. I., Part 2, containing St. John and the Acts, 10s. 6d.
Vol. II., Part 1, containing the Epistles of St. Paul, with a Map. 16s.

Alford's (Dean) Sermons on Christian Doctrine, preached in Canterbury Cathedral, on the Afternoons of the Sundays in the year 1861-62. Second Edition. Crown 8vo. 7s. 6d.

Alford's (Dean) Sermons preached at Quebec Chapel, 1854 to 1857. In Seven Volumes, small 8vo. 2l. 1s.

Sold separately as follows:—

Vols. I. and II. (A course for the Year.) Second Edition. 12s. 6d.
Vol. III. (On Practical Subjects.) 7s. 6d.
Vol. IV. (On Divine Love.) Third Edition. 5s.
Vol. V. (On Christian Practice.) Second Edition. 5s.
Vol. VI. (On the Person and Office of Christ.) 5s.
Vol. VII. (Concluding Series.) 6s.

Anderson's (Hon. Mrs.) Practical Religion exemplified, by Letters and Passages from the Life of the late Rev. Robert Anderson, of Brighton. Sixth Edition. Small 8vo. 4s.

Annual Register; a Review of Public Events at Home and Abroad, for the Years 1863 and 1864; being the First and Second Volumes of an improved Series. 8vo. 18s. each.

Arnold's School Series (see page 18).

Arnold's (Rev. T. K.) Sermons preached in a Country Village. Post 8vo. 5s. 6d.

Arnold's (Rev. Dr. T.) History of Rome, from the Earliest Period to the End of the Second Punic War. New Edition. 3 vols. 8vo. 36s.

Arnold's (Rev. Dr. T.) History of the later Roman Commonwealth, from the End of the Second Punic War to the Death of Julius Cæsar, with the Reign of Augustus, and a Life of Trajan. New Edition. 2 vols. 8vo. 24s.

Articles (The) of the Christian Faith, considered in reference to the Duties and Privileges of Christ's Church Militant here on Earth. Small 8vo. 3s. 6d.

Beaven's (Rev. Dr.) Questions on Scripture History. Fourth Edition, revised. 18mo. 2s.

Beaven's (Rev. Dr.) Help to Catechising; for the use of Clergymen, Schools, and Private Families. New Edition. 18mo. 2s.

Bethell's (Bishop) General View of the Doctrine of Regeneration in Baptism. Fifth Edition. 8vo. 9s.

Bickersteth's (Archdeacon) Questions illustrating the Thirty-nine Articles of the Church of England: with Proofs from Scripture and the Primitive Church. Fifth Edition. 12mo. 3s. 6d.

Bickersteth's (Archdeacon) Catechetical Exercises on the Apostles' Creed; chiefly drawn from the Exposition of Bishop Pearson. New Edition. 18mo. 2s.

Blunt's (Rev. J. H.) Directorium Pastorale: the Principles and Practice of Pastoral Work in the Church of England. Crown 8vo. 9s.

This work has been written with the object of providing for Theological students and the younger Clergy a Practical Manual on the subject of which it treats.

Contents:—Chap. I. The nature of the Pastoral Office.—Chap. II. The relation of the Pastor to God.—Chap. III. The relation of the Pastor to his flock.—Chap. IV. The ministry of God's Word.—Chap. V. The ministry of the Sacraments, &c.—Chap. VI. The Visitation of the Sick.—Chap. VII. Pastoral converse.—Chap. VIII. Private Instruction.—Chap. IX. Schools.—Chap. X. Parochial lay co-operation.—Chap. XI. Auxiliary Parochial Institutions.—Chap. XII. Parish Festivals.—Chap. XIII. Miscellaneous Responsibilities.

Blunt's (Rev. J. H) Household Theology; a Handbook of Religious Information respecting the Holy Bible, the Prayer Book, the Church, the Ministry, Divine Worship, the Creeds, &c., &c. Small 8vo. 6s.

Boyle's (W. R. A.) Inspiration of the Book of Daniel, and other portions of Sacred Scripture. With a correction of Profane, and an adjustment of Sacred Chronology. 8vo. 14s.

Bright's (Rev. W.) Faith and Life; Readings for the greater Holydays, and the Sundays from Advent to Trinity. Compiled from Ancient Writers. Small 8vo. 5s.

Brown's (Rev. G. J.) Lectures on the Gospel according to St. John, in the form of a Continuous Commentary. 2 vols. 8vo. 24s.

Browne's (Sir Thomas) Christian Morals. With a Life of the Author by Samuel Johnson. In small 8vo. with Portrait of Author, price 6s. handsomely printed on toned paper from antique type.

Burke.—A Complete Edition of the Works and Correspondence of the Right Hon. Edmund Burke. In 8 vols. 8vo. *With Portrait.* 4l. 4s.

Contents:—1. Mr. Burke's Correspondence between the year 1744 and his Decease in 1797, first published from the original MSS. in 1844, edited by Earl Fitzwilliam and Sir Richard Bourke. The most interesting portion of the Letters of Mr. Burke to Dr. French Laurence is also included in it.

2. The Works of Mr. Burke, as edited by his Literary Executors, and completed by the publication of the 15th and 16th Volumes, in 1826, under the Superintendence of the late Bishop of Rochester, Dr. Walker King.

Burke's (Edmund) Reflections on the Revolution in France, in 1790. New Edition, with a short Biographical Notice. 8vo. 4s. 6d.

Cambridge Year-Book and University Almanack for 1865. Edited by William White, Sub-Librarian of Trinity College. Crown 8vo. 2s. 6d. sewed; or, 3s. 6d. in cloth.

Caswall's (Rev. Dr.) Martyr of the Pongas. A Memoir of the Rev. Hamble James Leacock, first West-Indian Missionary to Western Africa. Small 8vo. With Portrait. 5s. 6d.

Chase's (Rev. D. P.) Translation of the Nicomachean Ethics of Aristotle; with an Introduction, a Marginal Analysis, and Explanatory Notes. Designed for the use of Students in the Universities. Second Edition, revised. Crown 8vo. 6s.

Christian's (The) Duty, from the Sacred Scriptures. In Two Parts. [*London: sold by C. Rivington, in St. Paul's Churchyard.* 1730.] New Edition. Edited by the Rev. Thomas Dale, M.A. Small 8vo. (1852.) 5s.

Clergy Charities.—List of Charities, General and Diocesan, for the Relief of the Clergy, their Widows and Families. Fifth Edition. Small 8vo. 3s.

Clissold's (Rev. H.) Lamps of the Church; or, Rays of
Faith, Hope, and Charity, from the Lives and Deaths of some Eminent
Christians of the Nineteenth Century. *New and cheaper Edition.* Crown
8vo., with five Portraits. 5s.

Codd's (Rev. A.) The Fifty-Third Chapter of Isaiah. A
Course of Lectures, delivered in Holy Week and on Easter Day, in the
Parish Church of Beaminster, Dorset. Small 8vo. 3s. 6d.

Cotterill's Selection of Psalms and Hymns for Public Worship. New and cheaper Editions. 32mo., 1s.; in 18mo. (large print),
1s. 6d. Also an Edition on fine paper, 2s. 6d.

₊ A large allowance to Clergymen and Churchwardens.

Cox's (Miss) Hymns from the German; accompanied by the
German originals. Second Edition, elegantly printed in small 8vo. 5s.

Cox's (Rev. J. M.) The Church on the Rock: or, the Claims
and some Distinctive Doctrines of the Church of Rome considered, in Six
Lectures. Small 8vo. 3s.

Coxe's (Archdeacon) Plain Thoughts on Important Church
Subjects. Small 8vo. 3s.

Crosthwaite's (Rev. J. C.) Historical Passages and Characters in the Book of Daniel; Eight Lectures, delivered in 1852, at the
Lecture founded by the late Bernard Hyde, Esq. To which are added,
Four Discourses on Mutual Recognition in a Future State. 12mo.
7s. 6d.

Daily Service Hymnal. 12mo., 1s. 6d. 32mo., 6d.

Davys's (Bp. of Peterborough) Plain and Short History of
England for Children: in Letters from a Father to his Son. With Questions. Fourteenth and Cheaper Edition. 18mo. 1s. 6d.

Denton's (Rev. W.) Commentary, Practical and Exegetical,
on the Lord's Prayer. Small 8vo. 5s.

Elliott's (Rev. H. Venn) Sermons at Cambridge, 1850-54.
Crown 8vo. 7s.

Ellison's (Rev. H. J.) Way of Holiness in Married Life;
Course of Sermons preached in Lent. Second Edition. Small 8vo.
2s. 6d. *In white cloth, antique style*, 3s. 6d.

Englishman's (The) Magazine of Literature, Religion, Science,
and Art. Vol. I., January to June, 1865. 8vo. 7s. 6d.

Espin's (Rev. T. E.) Critical Essays. Crown 8vo. 7s. 6d.
Contents :—Wesleyan Methodism—Essays and Reviews—Edward
Irving—Sunday—Bishop Wilson, of Sodor and Man—Bishop Wilson, of
Calcutta—Calvin.

Evans's (Rev. R. W.) Bishopric of Souls. Fourth Edition. Small 8vo. 5s.

Evans's (Rev. R. W.) Ministry of the Body. Second Edition. Small 8vo. 6s. 6d.

Exton's (Rev. R. B.) Speculum Gregis; or, the Parochial Minister's Assistant in the Oversight of his Flock. With blank forms to be filled up at discretion. Seventh Edition. In pocket size. 4s. 6d. bound with clasp.

Fearon's (Rev. H.) Sermons on Public Subjects. Small 8vo. 3s. 6d.

Fulford's (Bp. of Montreal) Sermons, Addresses, and Statistics of the Diocese. 8vo. 5s.

Gilly's (Rev. Canon) Memoir of Felix Neff, Pastor of the High Alps; and of his Labours among the French Protestants of Dauphiné, a Remnant of the Primitive Christians of Gaul. Sixth Edition. Fcap. 5s. 6d.

Girdlestone's (Rev. Charles) Holy Bible, containing the Old and New Testaments; with a Commentary arranged in Short Lectures for the Daily Use of Families. New Edition, in 6 vols. 8vo. 3l. 3s.
The Old Testament separately. 4 vols. 8vo. 42s.
The New Testament. 2 vols. 8vo. 21s.

Goulburn's (Rev. Dr.) Thoughts on Personal Religion. Eighth Edition, revised and enlarged. Small 8vo. 6s. 6d.

Goulburn's (Rev. Dr.) Office of the Holy Communion in the Book of Common Prayer; a Series of Lectures delivered in the Church of St. John the Evangelist, Paddington. Third Edition. Small 8vo. 6s.

Goulburn's (Rev. Dr.) Sermons preached on Various Occasions during the last Twenty Years. Second Edition. 2 vols. small 8vo. 10s. 6d.

Goulburn's (Rev. Dr.) The Idle Word: Short Religious Essays upon the Gift of Speech, and its Employment in Conversation. Third Edition. Small 8vo. 3s.

Goulburn's (Rev. Dr.) Introduction to the Devotional Study of the Holy Scriptures. Seventh Edition. Small 8vo. 3s. 6d.

Goulburn's (Rev. Dr.) Family Prayers, arranged on the Liturgical Principle. Third Edition. Small 8vo. 3s.

Goulburn's (Rev. Dr.) Short Devotional Forms, compiled to meet the Exigencies of a Busy life. New Edition, elegantly printed in square 16mo. 1s. 6d.

Goulburn's (Rev. Dr.) Manual of Confirmation. Fifth Edition. 1s. 6d.

MESSRS. RIVINGTON'S CATALOGUE. 7

Gould's (Rev. S. B.) Post-Mediæval Preachers. Post 8vo. 7s.

Gray's (Rev. J. B.) Psalter, Festival and Ferial, pointed and adapted to the Gregorian Tones. Crown 8vo. 4s.

Greswell's (Rev. Edward) The Three Witnesses and the Threefold Cord; being the Testimony of the Natural Measures of Time, of the Primitive Civil Calendar, and of Antediluvian and Postdiluvian Tradition, on the Principal Questions of Fact in Sacred or Profane Antiquity. 8vo. 7s. 6d.

Greswell's (Rev. Edward) Objections to the Historical Character of the Pentateuch, in Part I. of Dr. Colenso's " Pentateuch and Book of Joshua," considered, and shown to be unfounded. 8vo. 5s.

Greswell's (Rev. Edward) Exposition of the Parables and of other Parts of the Gospels. 5 vols. (in 6 parts), 8vo. 3l. 12s.

Grotius de Veritate Religionis Christianæ. With English Notes and Illustrations, for the use of Students. By the Rev. J. E. Middleton, M.A., of Trinity College, Cambridge; Lecturer on Theology at St. Bees' College. Second Edition. 12mo. 6s.

Gurney's (Rev. J. H.) Sermons on the Acts of the Apostles. With a Preface by the Dean of Canterbury. Small 8vo. 7s.

Gurney's (Rev. J. H.) Sermons chiefly on Old Testament Histories, from Texts in the Sunday Lessons. Second Edition. 6s.

Gurney's (Rev. J. H.) Sermons on Texts from the Epistles and Gospels for Twenty Sundays. Second Edition. 6s.

Gurney's (Rev. J. H.) Miscellaneous Sermons. 6s.

Hale's (Archdeacon) Sick Man's Guide to Acts of Faith, Patience, Charity, and Repentance. Extracted from Bishop Taylor's Holy Dying. In large print. Second Edition. 8vo. 3s.

Hall's (Rev. W. J.) Psalms and Hymns adapted to the Services of the Church of England; with a Supplement of additional Hymns and Indices. In 8vo., 5s. 6d.—18mo., 3s.—24mo., 1s. 6d.—24mo., limp cloth, 1s. 3d.—32mo., 1s.—32mo., limp, 8d. (The Supplement may be had separately.)

₊ A Prospectus of the above, with Specimens of Type, and farther particulars, may be had of the Publishers.

Hall's Selection of Psalms and Hymns; with Accompanying Tunes, selected and arranged by John Foster, of Her Majesty's Chapels Royal. Crown 8vo., *limp cloth*, 2s. 6d. The Tunes only, 1s.

Hall's Selection. An Edition of the above Tunes for the Organ. Oblong 8vo. 7s. 6d.

Help and Comfort for the Sick Poor. By the Author of
"Sickness: its Trials and Blessings." Fourth Edition, *in large print.*
1s., *or* 1s. 6d. *in cloth.*

Henley's (Hon. and Rev. R.) Sermons on the Beatitudes,
preached at St. Mary's Church, Putney. Small 8vo. 3s.

Henley's (Hon. and Rev. R.) The Prayer of Prayers.
Small 8vo. 4s. 6d.

Hessey's (Rev. Dr.) Biographies of the Kings of Judah:
Twelve Lectures. Crown 8vo. 6s. 6d.

Heygate's (Rev. W. E.) Care of the Soul; or, Sermons
on Points of Christian Prudence. 12mo. 5s. 6d.

Heygate's (Rev. W. E.) The Good Shepherd; or, Christ
the Pattern, Priest, and Pastor. 18mo. 3s. 6d.

Hodgson's (Chr.) Instructions for the Use of Candidates for
Holy Orders, and of the Parochial Clergy, as to Ordination, Licences,
Induction, Pluralities, Residence, &c. &c.; with Acts of Parliament relating to the above, and Forms to be used. Eighth Edition, revised and corrected. 8vo. 12s.

Holden's (Rev. Geo.) Ordinance of Preaching investigated.
Small 8vo. 3s. 6d.

Holden's (Rev. Geo.) Christian Expositor; or, Practical
Guide to the Study of the New Testament. Intended for the use of
General Readers. Second Edition. 12mo. 12s.

Hook's (Dean) Book of Family Prayer. Seventh Edition,
revised and enlarged. 18mo. 2s.

Hook's (Dean) Private Prayers. Fifth Edition. 18mo. 2s.

Hook's (Dean) Dictionary of Ecclesiastical Biography.
8 vols. 12mo. 2l. 11s.

Hours (The) of the Passion; with Devotional Forms for
Private and Household Use. 12mo. 5s. in limp cloth, or 6s. in cloth,
red edges.

Hulton's (Rev. C. G.) Catechetical Help to Bishop Butler's
Analogy. Third Edition. Post 8vo. 4s. 6d.

Hymns and Poems for the Sick and Suffering; in connexion
with the Service for the Visitation of the Sick. Selected from
various Authors. Edited by the Rev. T. V. Fosbery, M.A., Vicar of
St. Giles's, Reading. Sixth Edition. 5s. 6d. *in cloth, or* 9s. 6d. *in morocco.*

Jackson's (Bp. of Lincoln) Six Sermons on the Christian
Character; preached in Lent. Seventh Edition. Small 8vo. 3s. 6d.

James's (Rev. Dr.) Comment upon the Collects appointed
to be used in the Church of England on Sundays and Holydays throughout the Year. Fifteenth Edition. 12mo. 5s.

James's (Rev. Dr.) Christian Watchfulness in the Prospect of Sickness, Mourning, and Death. Eighth Edition. 12mo. 6s.
Cheap Editions of these two works may be had, price 3s. each.

James's (Rev. Dr.) Evangelical Life, as seen in the Example of our Lord Jesus Christ. Second Edition. 12mo. 7s. 6d.

James's (Rev. Dr.) Devotional Comment on the Morning and Evening Services in the Book of Common Prayer, in a Series of Plain Lectures. Second Edition. In 2 vols. 12mo. 10s. 6d.

Inman's (Rev. Professor) Treatise on Navigation and Nautical Astronomy, for the Use of British Seamen. Thirteenth Edition, edited by the Rev. J. W. Inman. Royal 8vo. 7s.

Inman's (Rev. Professor) Nautical Tables for the Use of British Seamen. New Edition, edited by the Rev. J. W. Inman. Royal 8vo. 14s.   Or, with a new Table of Latitudes and Longitudes, 16s.

Jones's (Rev. Harry) Life in the World: Sermons at St. Luke's, Berwick Street. Small 8vo. 5s.

Kaye's (Bishop) Account of the Writings and Opinions of Justin Martyr. Third Edition. 8vo. 7s. 6d.

Kaye's (Bishop) Ecclesiastical History of the Second and Third Centuries, Illustrated from the Writings of Tertullian. Third Edition. 8vo. 13s.

Kaye's (Bishop) Account of the Writings and Opinions of Clement of Alexandria. 8vo. 12s.

Kaye's (Bishop) Account of the Council of Nicæa, in connexion with the Life of Athanasius. 8vo. 8s.

Kennaway's (Rev. C. E.) Consolatio; or, Comfort for the Afflicted. Selected from various Authors. With a Preface by the Bishop of Oxford. Eleventh Edition. Small 8vo. 4s. 6d.

Knowles's (Rev. E. H.) Notes on the Epistle to the Hebrews, with Analysis and Brief Paraphrase; for Theological Students. Crown 8vo. 6s. 6d.

Lee's (Archdeacon) Eight Discourses on the Inspiration of Holy Scripture. Fourth Edition. 8vo. 15s.

Lee's (Rev. F. G.) The Words from the Cross: Seven Sermons for Lent and Passion-tide. Second Edition. Small 8vo. 2s. 6d.

Lewis's (Rev. W. S.) Threshold of Revelation; or, Some Inquiry into the Province and True Character of the First Chapter of Genesis. Crown 8vo. 6s.

A 5

London Diocese Book for 1865: containing an account of the See and its Bishops; of St. Paul's Cathedral, Westminster Abbey, and the Chapels Royal; of the Rural Deaneries, Foreign Chaplaincies, &c. By John Hassard, Private Secretary to the Bishop of London. Second Edition. Crown 8vo. 2s. 6d.

McCaul's (Rev. Dr.) Examination of Bp. Colenso's Difficulties with regard to the Pentateuch; and some Reasons for believing in its Authenticity and Divine Origin. Third Library Edition. Crown 8vo. 5s.

McCaul's (Rev. Dr.) Examination of Bp. Colenso's Difficulties with regard to the Pentateuch. Part II. Crown 8vo. 2s.

Mackenzie's (Rev. H.) Ordination Lectures, delivered in Rischolme Palace Chapel, during Ember Weeks. Small 8vo. 3s.
Contents:—Pastoral Government—Educational Work—Self-government in the Pastor—Missions and their Reflex Results—Dissent—Public Teaching—Sunday Schools—Doctrinal Controversy—Secular Aids.

Mansel's (Rev. Professor) Artis Logicæ Rudimenta, from the Text of Aldrich; with Notes and Marginal References. Fourth Edition, corrected and enlarged. 8vo. 10s. 6d.

Mansel's (Rev. Professor) Prolegomena Logica; an Inquiry into the Psychological Character of Logical Processes. Second Edition. 8vo. 10s. 6d.

Mant's (Bishop) Book of Common Prayer and Administration of the Sacraments, with copious Notes, Practical and Historical, from approved Writers of the Church of England; including the Canons and Constitutions of the Church. New Edition. In one volume, super-royal 8vo. 24s.

Mant's (Bishop) Happiness of the Blessed considered as to the Particulars of their State; their Recognition of each other in that State; and its Difference of Degrees. Seventh Edition. 12mo. 4s.

Margaret Stourton; or, a Year of Governess Life. Elegantly printed in small 8vo. Price 5s.

Marriott's (Rev. Wharton B.) Adelphi of Terence, with English Notes. Small 8vo. 3s.

Marsh's (Bishop) Comparative View of the Churches of England and Rome: with an Appendix on Church Authority, the Character of Schism, and the Rock on which our Saviour declared that He would build His Church. Third Edition. Small 8vo. 6s.

Massingberd's (Rev. F. C.) Lectures on the Prayer-Book. Small 8vo. 3s. 6d.

Mayd's (Rev. W.) Sunday Evening; or, a Short and Plain Exposition of the Gospel for every Sunday in the Year. Crown 8vo. 5s.

Medd's (Rev. P. G.) Household Prayer; with Morning and Evening Readings for a Month. Small 8vo. 4s. 6d.

Melvill's (Rev. H.) Sermons. Vol. I., Sixth Edition. Vol. II., Fourth Edition. 10s. 6d. each.

Melvill's (Rev. H.) Sermons on some of the less prominent Facts and References in Sacred Story. Second Series. 8vo. 10s. 6d.

Melvill's (Rev. H.) Selection from the Lectures delivered at St. Margaret's, Lothbury, on the Tuesday Mornings in the Years 1850, 1851, 1852. Small 8vo. 6s.

Middleton's (Bp.) Doctrine of the Greek Article applied to the Criticism and Illustration of the New Testament. With Prefatory Observations and Notes, by Hugh James Rose, B.D., late Principal of King's College, London. New Edition. 8vo. 12s.

Mill's (Rev. Dr.) Analysis of Bishop Pearson on the Creed. Third Edition. 8vo. 5s.

Miller's (Rev. J. K.) Parochial Sermons. Small 8vo. 4s. 6d.

Missing Doctrine (The) in Popular Preaching. Small 8vo. 5s.

Monsell's (Rev. Dr.) Parish Musings; or, Devotional Poems. Eighth Edition, elegantly printed on toned paper. Small 8vo. 2s. 6d.

Also, a CHEAP EDITION, price 1s. sewed, or 1s. 6d. in limp cloth.

Moore's (Rev. Daniel) The Age and the Gospel; Four Sermons preached before the University of Cambridge, at the Hulsean Lecture, 1864. Crown 8vo. 5s.

Moreton's (Rev. Julian) Life and Work in Newfoundland: Reminiscences of Thirteen Years spent there. Crown 8vo., *with a Map and four Illustrations.* 5s. 6d.

Mozley's (Rev. J. B.) Review of the Baptismal Controversy. 8vo. 9s. 6d.

Nixon's (Bishop) Lectures, Historical, Doctrinal, and Practical, on the Catechism of the Church of England. Sixth Edition. 8vo. 18s.

Notes on Wild Flowers. By a Lady. Small 8vo. 9s.

Old Man's (The) Rambles. Sixth and cheaper Edition. 18mo. 3s. 6d.

Parkinson's (Canon) Old Church Clock. Fourth Edition. Small 8vo. 4s. 6d.

Parry's (Mrs.) Young Christian's Sunday Evening; or, Conversations on Scripture History. In 3 vols. small 8vo. Sold separately:
First Series: on the Old Testament. Fourth Edition. 6s. 6d.
Second Series: on the Gospels. Third Edition. 7s.
Third Series: on the Acts. Second Edition. 4s. 6d.

Parry's (Rev. E. St. John) School Sermons preached at Leamington College. Small 8vo. 4s. 6d.

Peile's (Rev. Dr.) Annotations on the Apostolical Epistles. New Edition. 4 vols. 8vo. 42s.

Pepys's (Lady C.) Quiet Moments: a Four Weeks' Course of Thoughts and Meditations before Evening Prayer and at Sunset. Fourth Edition. Small 8vo. 3s. 6d.

Pepys's (Lady C.) Morning Notes of Praise: a Companion Volume. Second Edition. 3s. 6d.

Pepys's (Lady C.) Thoughts for the Hurried and Hardworking. Second Edition, in large print, price 1s. sewed, or 1s. 6d. in limp cloth.

Physical Science compared with the Second Beast of the Revelations. Small 8vo. 3s. 6d.

Pigou's (Rev. Francis) Faith and Practice; Sermons at St. Philip's, Regent Street. Small 8vo. 6s.

Pinder's (Rev. Canon) Sermons on the Book of Common Prayer and Administration of the Sacraments. To which are now added, Several Sermons on the Feasts and Fasts of the Church, preached in the Cathedral Church of Wells. Third Edition. 12mo. 7s.

Pinder's (Rev. Canon) Sermons on the Holy Days observed in the Church of England throughout the Year. Second Edition. 12mo. 6s. 6d.

Pinder's (Rev. Canon) Meditations and Prayers on the Ordination Service for Deacons. Small 8vo. 3s. 6d.

Pinder's (Rev. Canon) Meditations and Prayers on the Ordination Service for Priests. Small 8vo. 3s. 6d.

Plain Sermons. By Contributors to the "Tracts for the Times." In 10 vols. 8vo., 6s. 6d. each. (Sold separately.)
This Series contains 347 original Sermons of moderate length, written in simple language, and in an earnest and impressive style, forming a copious body of practical Theology, in accordance with the Doctrines of the Church of England. They are particularly suited for family reading. The last Volume contains a general Index of Subjects, and a Table of the Sermons adapted to the various Seasons of the Christian Year.

Prayers for the Sick and Dying. By the Author of " Sickness, its Trials and Blessings." Fourth Edition. Small 8vo. 2s. 6d.

Prichard's (Rev. C. E.) Commentary on Ephesians, Philippians, and Colossians, for English Readers. Crown 8vo. 4s. 6d.

Priest (The) to the Altar; or, Aids to the Devout Celebration of Holy Communion, chiefly after the Ancient English Use of Sarum. 8vo. 7s. 6d.

Public Schools (The) Calendar for 1865. Edited by a Graduate of the University of Oxford. Small 8vo. 6s.

₊ This Work is intended to furnish Annually an account of the Foundations and Endowments of the Schools: of the Course of Study and Discipline; Scholarships and Exhibitions; Fees and other Expenses; School Prizes and University Honours; Recreations and Vacations; Religious Instruction; and other useful information.

Pusey's (Rev. Dr.) Commentary on the Minor Prophets: with Introductions to the several Books. In 4to.
Parts I., II., III., price 5s. each, are already published.

Pusey's (Rev. Dr.) Daniel the Prophet; Nine Lectures delivered in the Divinity School. Third Thousand. 8vo. 12s.

Pusey's (Rev. Dr.) Letter to Rev. J. Keble on the Restoration of Unity in the Church. 8vo. 7s. 6d.

Reminiscences by a Clergyman's Wife. Edited by the Dean of Canterbury. Second Edition. Crown 8vo. 3s. 6d.

Sargent's (J. Y.) Outlines of Norwegian Grammar, with Exercises. Small 8vo. 3s.

Schmitz's (Dr. L.) Manual of Ancient History, from the Remotest Times to the Overthrow of the Western Empire, A.D. 476. Third Edition. Crown 8vo. 7s. 6d.

This Work, for the convenience of Schools, may be had in Two Parts, sold separately, viz.:—

Vol. I., containing, besides the History of India and the other Asiatic Nations, a complete History of Greece. 4s.

Vol. II., containing a complete History of Rome. 4s.

Schmitz's (Dr. L.) Manual of Ancient Geography. Crown 8vo. 6s.

Schmitz's (Dr. L.) History of the Middle Ages, from the Downfall of the Western Empire, A.D. 476, to the Crusades, A.D. 1096. Crown 8vo. 7s. 6d.

Scripture Record of the Life and Times of Samuel the Prophet. By the Author of "Scripture Record of the Blessed Virgin." Small 8vo. 3s.

Seymour's (Rev. R.) and Mackarness's (Rev. J. F.) Eighteen
Years of a Clerical Meeting: being the Minutes of the Alcester Clerical
Association, from 1842 to 1860; with a Preface on the Revival of Ruridecanal Chapters. Crown 8vo. 6s. 6d.

Sickness, its Trials and Blessings. Seventh Edition. Small
8vo. 3s. 6d. Also, a cheaper Edition, for distribution, 2s. 6d.

Slade's (Rev. Canon) Twenty-one Prayers composed from
the Psalms for the Sick and Afflicted: with other Forms of Prayer, and
Hints and Directions for the Visitation of the Sick. Seventh Edition.
12mo. 3s. 6d.

Slade's (Rev. Canon) Plain Parochial Sermons. 7 vols. 12mo.
6s. each. Sold separately.

Smith's (Rev. J. G.) Life of Our Blessed Saviour: an
Epitome of the Gospel Narrative, arranged in order of time from the latest
Harmonies. With Introduction and Notes. Square 16mo. 2s.

Smith's (Rev. Dr. J. B.) Manual of the Rudiments of
Theology: containing an Abridgment of Tomline's Elements; an Analysis
of Paley's Evidences; a Summary of Pearson on the Creed; and a brief
Exposition of the Thirty-nine Articles, chiefly from Burnet; Explanation
of Jewish Rites and Ceremonies, &c. &c. Fifth Edition. 12mo. 8s. 6d.

Smith's (Rev. Dr. J. B.) Compendium of Rudiments in
Theology: containing a Digest of Bishop Butler's Analogy; an Epitome
of Dean Graves on the Pentateuch; and an Analysis of Bishop Newton
on the Prophecies. Second Edition. 12mo. 9s.

Stock's (Rev. John) Commentary on the First Epistle of
St. John. 8vo. 10s.

Talbot's (Hon. Mrs. J. C.) Parochial Mission-Women; their
Work and its Fruits. Second Edition. Small 8vo. In limp cloth, 2s.

Thornton's (Rev. T.) Life of Moses, in a Course of Village
Lectures; with a Preface Critical of Bishop Colenso's Work on the
Pentateuch. Small 8vo. 3s. 6d.

Threshold (The) of Private Devotion. Second Edition.
16mo. 2s.

Townsend's (Canon) Holy Bible, containing the Old and
New Testaments, arranged in Historical and Chronological Order. With
copious Notes and Indexes. Fifth Edition. In 2 vols., imperial 8vo.,
21s. each (sold separately).
Also, an Edition of this Arrangement of the Bible without the Notes,
in One Volume, 14s.

Trollope's (Rev. W.) Iliad of Homer from a carefully corrected Text; with copious English Notes, illustrating the Grammatical
Construction, the Manners and Customs, the Mythology and Antiquities
of the Heroic Ages: and Preliminary Observations on points of Classical
interest. Fifth Edition. 8vo. 15s.

Vidal's (Mrs.) Tales for the Bush. Originally published in Australia. Fourth Edition. Small 8vo. 5s.

Virgilii Æneidos Libri I—VI; with English Notes, chiefly from the Edition of P. Wagner, by T. Clayton, M.A., and C. S. Jerram, M.A. Small 8vo. 4s. 6d.

Warter's (Rev. J. W.) The Sea-board and the Down; or, My Parish in the South. In 2 vols. small 4to. Elegantly printed in Antique type, with Illustrations. 28s.

Webster's (Rev. W.) Syntax and Synonyms of the Greek Testament. 8vo. 9s.

The Syntax is based upon Donaldson's, with extracts from the writings of Archbishop Trench, Dean Alford, Dr. Wordsworth, but more especially from Bishop Ellicott, and the work on the Romans by Dr. Vaughan. Considerable use has also been made of the Article in the "Quarterly Review" for January, 1863.

The chapter on Synonyms treats of many words which have not been noticed by other writers. In another chapter attention is drawn to some passages in which the Authorized Version is incorrect, inexact, insufficient, or obscure. Copious Indices are added.

Welchman's Thirty-nine Articles of the Church of England, illustrated with Notes. New Edition. 2s. Or, interleaved with blank paper, 3s.

Wilberforce's (Bp. of Oxford) History of the Protestant Episcopal Church in America. Third Edition. Small 8vo. 5s.

Wilberforce's (Bp. of Oxford) Rocky Island, and other Similitudes. Twelfth Edition, with Cuts. 18mo. 2s. 6d.

Wilberforce's (Bp. of Oxford) Sermons preached before the Queen. Sixth Edition. 12mo. 6s.

Wilberforce's (Bp. of Oxford) Selection of Psalms and Hymns for Public Worship. New Edition. 32mo. 1s. each, or 3l. 10s. per hundred.

Williams's (Rev. Isaac) The Psalms interpreted of Christ; a Devotional Commentary. Vol. I. Small 8vo. 7s. 6d.

Williams's (Rev. Isaac) Devotional Commentary on the Gospel Narrative. 8 vols. small 8vo. 3l. 6s.

Sold separately as follows:—
  Thoughts on the Study of the Gospels. 8s.
  Harmony of the Evangelists. 8s. 6d.
 The Nativity (extending to the Calling of St. Matthew). 8s. 6d.
  Second Year of the Ministry. 8s.
  Third Year of the Ministry. 8s. 6d.
 The Holy Week. 8s. 6d.   The Passion. 8s.
  The Resurrection. 8s.

Williams's (Rev. Isaac) Apocalypse, with Notes and Reflections. Small 8vo. 8s. 6d.

Williams's (Rev. Isaac) Beginning of the Book of Genesis, with Notes and Reflections. Small 8vo. 7s. 6d.

Williams's (Rev. Isaac) Sermons on the Characters of the Old Testament. Second Edition. 5s. 6d.

Williams's (Rev. Isaac) Female Characters of Holy Scripture; in a Series of Sermons. Second Edition. Small 8vo. 5s. 6d.

Williams's (Rev. Isaac) Plain Sermons on the Latter Part of the Catechism; being the Conclusion of the Series contained in the Ninth Volume of "Plain Sermons." 8vo. 6s. 6d.

Williams's (Rev. Isaac) Complete Series of Sermons on the Catechism. In one Volume. 13s.

Williams's (Rev. Isaac) Sermons on the Epistle and Gospel for the Sundays and Holy Days throughout the Year. Second Edition. In 3 vols. small 8vo. 16s. 6d.

✱ The Third Volume, on the Saints' Days and other Holy Days of the Church, may be had separately, price 5s. 6d.

Williams's (Rev. Isaac) Christian Seasons; a Series of Poems. Small 8vo. 3s. 6d.

Willis (Rev. W. D.) on Simony. New Edition. 8vo. 7s. 6d.

Wilson's (Rev. Plumpton) Meditations and Prayers for Persons in Private. Fourth Edition, elegantly printed in 18mo. 4s. 6d.

Wilson's (late Bp. of Sodor and Man) Short and Plain Instruction for the Better Understanding of the Lord's Supper. To which is annexed, The Office of the Holy Communion, with Proper Helps and Directions. Pocket size, 1s. Also, a larger Edition, 2s.

Wilson's (late Bp. of Sodor and Man) Sacra Privata; Private Meditations and Prayers. Pocket size, 1s. Also, a larger Edition, 2s.

These two Works may be had in various bindings.

Woodward's (Rev. F. B.) Tracts and Sermons on Subjects of the Day; with an Appendix on the Roman Catholic Controversy. 12mo. 7s.

Wordsworth's (late Rev. Dr.) Ecclesiastical Biography; or, Lives of Eminent Men connected with the History of Religion in England, from the Commencement of the Reformation to the Revolution. Selected, and Illustrated with Notes. Fourth Edition. In 4 vols. 8vo. With 5 Portraits. 2l. 14s.

Wordsworth's (Bp. of St. Andrew's) Christian Boyhood at a Public School: a Collection of Sermons and Lectures delivered at Winchester College from 1836 to 1846. In 2 vols. 8vo. 1l. 4s.

Wordsworth's (Bp. of St. Andrew's) Catechesis; or, Christian Instruction preparatory to Confirmation and First Communion. Third Edition. Crown 8vo. 3s. 6d.

Wordsworth's (Archd.) New Testament of our Lord and Saviour Jesus Christ, in the original Greek. With Notes, Introductions, and Indexes. New Edition. In Two Vols., imperial 8vo. 4l.

Separately,

Part I.: The Four Gospels. 1l. 1s.
Part II.: The Acts of the Apostles. 10s. 6d.
Part III.: The Epistles of St. Paul. 1l. 11s. 6d.
Part IV.: The General Epistles and Book of Revelation; with Indexes. 1l. 1s.

Wordsworth's (Archd.) The Holy Bible. With Notes and Introductions. Part I., containing Genesis and Exodus. Imperial 8vo. 21s. Part II., Leviticus to Deuteronomy. 18s.

Wordsworth's (Archd.) Occasional Sermons preached in Westminster Abbey. In 7 vols. 8vo. Vols. I., II., and III., 7s. each—Vols. IV. and V., 8s. each—Vol. VI., 7s.—Vol. VII., 6s.

Wordsworth's (Archd.) Theophilus Anglicanus; or, Instruction concerning the Principles of the Church Universal and the Church of England. Ninth Edition. Small 8vo. 5s.

Wordsworth's (Archd.) Elements of Instruction on the Church; being an Abridgment of the above. Second Edition. 2s.

Wordsworth's (Archd.) Journal of a Tour in Italy; with Reflections on the Present Condition and Prospects of Religion in that Country. Second Edition. 2 vols. post 8vo. 15s.

Wordsworth's (Archd.) On the Interpretation of the Bible. Five Lectures delivered at Westminster Abbey. 3s. 6d.

Wordsworth's (Archd.) Holy Year: Hymns for Sundays and Holydays, and for other Occasions; with a preface on Hymnology. Third Edition, in larger type, square 16mo., cloth extra, 4s. 6d.
Also an Edition with Tunes, 4s. 6d.; and a cheap Edition, 6d.

Worgan's (Rev. J. H.) Divine Week; or, Outlines of a Harmony of the Geologic Periods with the Mosaic "Days" of Creation. Crown 8vo. 5s.

Yonge's (C. D.) History of England from the Earliest Times to the Peace of Paris, 1856. With a Chronological Table of Contents. In one thick volume, crown 8vo. 12s.

Though available as a School-book, this volume contains as much as three ordinary octavos. It is written on a carefully digested plan, ample space being given to the last three centuries. All the best authorities have been consulted.

A

SELECTION FROM THE SCHOOL SERIES

OF THE

REV. THOMAS KERCHEVER ARNOLD, M.A.

LATE FELLOW OF TRINITY COLLEGE, CAMBRIDGE.

Practical Introductions to Greek, Latin, &c.

Henry's First Latin Book. Eighteenth Edition. 12mo. 3s.

The object of this work is to enable the youngest boys to master the principal difficulties of the Latin language by easy steps, and to furnish older students with a Manual for Self-Tuition.

Great attention has lately been given to the improvement of what may be called its mechanical parts. The Vocabularies have been much extended, and greater uniformity of reference has been secured. A few rules have been omitted or simplified. Every thing has been done which the long experience of the Editor, or the practice of his friends in their own schools has shown to be desirable.

At the same time, no pains have been spared to do this without altering in any way the character of the work, or making it inconvenient to use it side by side with copies of earlier editions.

Supplementary Exercises to Henry's First Latin Book. By G. B. Hill, B.A. 2s.

A Second Latin Book, and Practical Grammar. Intended as a Sequel to Henry's First Latin Book. Eighth Edition. 12mo. 4s.

A First Verse Book, Part I.; intended as an easy Introduction to the Latin Hexameter and Pentameter. Eighth Edition. 12mo. 2s.   Part II.; Additional Exercises. 1s.

Historiæ Antiquæ Epitome, from *Cornelius Nepos, Justin*, &c. With English Notes, Rules for Construing, Questions, Geographical Lists, &c. Seventh Edition. 4s.

A First Classical Atlas, containing fifteen Maps, coloured in outline; intended as a Companion to the *Historiæ Antiquæ Epitome*. 8vo. 7s. 6d.

A Practical Introduction to Latin Prose Composition. Part I. Thirteenth Edition. 8vo. 6s. 6d.

This Work is founded on the principles of imitation and frequent repetition. It is at once a Syntax, a Vocabulary, and an Exercise Book; and considerable attention has been paid to the subject of Synonymes. It is now used at all, or nearly all, the public schools.

A Practical Introduction to Latin Prose Composition, Part II.; containing the Doctrine of Latin Particles, with Vocabulary, an Antibarbarus, &c. Fourth Edition. 8vo. 8s.

A Practical Introduction to Latin Verse Composition. Fourth and Cheaper Edition, considerably revised. 12mo. 3s. 6d.

This Work supposes the pupil to be already capable of composing verses easily when the "*full sense*" is given. Its object is to facilitate his transition to original composition in Elegiacs and Hexameters, and to teach him to compose the Alcaic and Sapphic stanzas: explanations and a few exercises are also given on the other Horatian metres. A short Poetical Phraseology is added.

In the present Edition the whole work has been corrected, the translations being carefully compared with the originals. The Alcaics and Sapphics have been arranged in stanzas, and each kind of verse placed in a separate chapter, the old numbers of the Exercises being preserved for convenience in use. Other improvements have been made which it is hoped will add to its value.

Gradus ad Parnassum Novus Anticlepticus; founded on Quicherat's *Thesaurus Poeticus Linguæ Latinæ*. 8vo. half-bound. 10s. 6d.

*** A Prospectus, with specimen page, may be had of the Publishers.

Longer Latin Exercises, Part I. Third Edition. 8vo. 4s.

The object of this Work is to supply boys with an easy collection of *short* passages, as an Exercise Book for those who have gone once, at least, through the First Part of the Editor's " Practical Introduction to Latin Prose Composition."

Longer Latin Exercises, Part II.; containing a Selection of Passages of greater length, in genuine idiomatic English, for Translation into Latin. 8vo. 4s.

Materials for Translation into Latin: selected and arranged by Augustus Grotefend. Translated from the German by the Rev. H. H. Arnold, B.A., with Notes and Excursuses. Third Edition. 8vo. 7s. 6d.

A Copious and Critical English-Latin Lexicon, by the Rev. T. K. Arnold and the Rev. J. E. Riddle. Sixth Edition. 1l. 5s.

An Abridgment of the above Work, for the Use of Schools. By the Rev. J. C. Ebden, late Fellow and Tutor of Trinity Hall, Cambridge. Square 12mo. *bound*. 10s. 6d.

The First Greek Book; on the Plan of " Henry's First Latin Book." Fifth Edition. 12mo. 5s.

The Second Greek Book (on the same Plan); containing an Elementary Treatise on the Greek Particles and the Formation of Greek Derivatives. 12mo. 5s. 6d.

A Practical Introduction to Greek Accidence. With Easy
Exercises and Vocabulary. Seventh Edition. 8vo. 5s. 6d.

A Practical Introduction to Greek Prose Composition, Part I.
Tenth Edition. 8vo. 5s. 6d.

The object of this Work is to enable the Student, as soon as he can decline and conjugate with tolerable facility, to translate simple sentences after given examples, and with given words; the principles trusted to being principally those of *imitation and very frequent repetition*. It is at once a Syntax, a Vocabulary, and an Exercise Book.

Professor Madvig's Syntax of the Greek Language, especially
of the Attic Dialect; translated by the Rev. Henry Browne, M.A.
Together with an Appendix on the Greek Particles; by the Translator.
Square 8vo. 8s. 6d.

An Elementary Greek Grammar. 12mo. 5s.; or, with
Dialects, 6s.

A Complete Greek and English Lexicon for the Poems of
Homer, and the Homeridæ. Translated from the German of Crusius,
by Professor Smith. New and Revised Edition. 9s. *half-bound*.

*** A Prospectus and specimen of this Lexicon may be had.

A Copious Phraseological English-Greek Lexicon, founded
on a work prepared by J. W. Frädersdorff, Ph. Dr. of the Taylor-Institution, Oxford. Revised, Enlarged, and Improved by the Rev. T. K. Arnold, M.A., formerly Fellow of Trinity College, Cambridge, and Henry Browne, M.A., Vicar of Pevensey, and Prebendary of Chichester. Third Edition, corrected, with the Appendix incorporated. 8vo. 21s.

*** A Prospectus, with specimen page, may be had.

Classical Examination Papers. A Series of 93 Extracts
from Greek, Roman, and English Classics for Translation, with occasional
Questions and Notes; each extract on a separate leaf. Price of the whole
in a specimen packet, 4s., or six copies of any Separate Paper may be had
for 3d.

Keys to the following may be had by Tutors only:

First Latin Book, 1s.   Second Latin Book, 2s.
     Cornelius Nepos, 1s.
First Verse Book, 1s.   Latin Verse Composition, 2s.
     Latin Prose Composition, Parts I. and II., 1s. 6d. each.
Longer Latin Exercises, Part I., 1s. 6d.   Part II., 2s. 6d.
     Greek Prose Composition, Part I., 1s. 6d.   Part II., 4s. 6d.
         First Greek Book, 1s. 6d.   Second, 2s.

ARNOLD'S SCHOOL SERIES.   21

The First Hebrew Book; on the Plan of "Henry's First Latin Book." 12mo. Second Edition. 7s. 6d.   The Key. Second Edition. 3s. 6d.

The Second Hebrew Book, containing the Book of Genesis; together with a Hebrew Syntax, and a Vocabulary and Grammatical Commentary. 9s.

The First German Book; on the Plan of "Henry's First Latin Book." By the Rev. T. K. Arnold and Dr. Frädersdorff. Fifth Edition. 12mo. 5s. 6d.   The Key, 2s. 6d.

A Reading Companion to the First German Book; containing Extracts from the best Authors with a Vocabulary and Notes. 12mo. Second Edition. 4s.

The First French Book; on the Plan of "Henry's First Latin Book." Fifth Edition. 12mo. 5s. 6d.   Key to the Exercises, by Delille, 2s. 6d.

Henry's English Grammar; a Manual for Beginners. 12mo. 3s. 6d.

Spelling turned Etymology. Second Edition. 12mo. 2s. 6d.

The Pupil's Book, (a Companion to the above,) 1s. 3d.

Latin viâ English; being the Second Part of the above Work. Second Edition. 12mo. 4s. 6d.

An English Grammar for Classical Schools; being a Practical Introduction to "English Prose Composition." Sixth Edition. 12mo. 4s. 6d.

Handbooks for the Classical Student, with Questions.

Ancient History and Geography. Translated from the German of Pütz, by the Ven. Archdeacon Paul. Second Edition. 12mo. 6s. 6d.

Mediæval History and Geography. Translated from the German of Pütz. By the same. 12mo. 4s. 6d.

Modern History and Geography. Translated from the German of Pütz. By the same. 12mo. 5s. 6d.

Grecian Antiquities. By Professor Bojesen. Translated
from the German Version of Dr. Hoffa. By the same. Second Edition.
12mo. 3s. 6d.

Roman Antiquities. By Professor Bojesen. Second Edition.
3s. 6d.

Hebrew Antiquities. By the Rev. Henry Browne, M.A.
Prebendary of Chichester. 12mo. 4s.

*** This Work describes the manners and customs of the ancient Hebrews which were common to them with other nations, and the rites and ordinances which distinguished them as the chosen people Israel.

Greek Synonymes. From the French of Pillon. 6s. 6d.

Latin Synonymes. From the German of Döderlein. Translated by the Rev. H. H. Arnold. Second Edition. 4s.

Arnold's School Classics.

Cornelius Nepos, Part I.; with Critical Questions and Answers, and an imitative Exercise on each Chapter. Fourth Edition. 12mo. 4s.

Eclogæ Ovidianæ, with English Notes; Part I. (from the Elegiac Poems.) Tenth Edition. 12mo. 2s. 6d.

Eclogæ Ovidianæ, Part II. (from the Metamorphoses.) 5s.

The Æneid of Virgil, with English Notes. 12mo. 6s.

The Works of Horace, followed by English Introductions and Notes, adapted for School use. 12mo. 7s.

Cicero.—Selections from his Orations, with English Notes, from the best and most recent sources. Contents:—The Fourth Book of the Impeachment of Verres, the Four Speeches against Catiline, and the Speech for the Poet Archias. Second Edition. 12mo. 4s.

Cicero, Part II.; containing Selections from his Epistles, arranged in the order of time, with Accounts of the Consuls, Events of each year, &c. With English Notes from the best Commentators, especially Matthiæ. 12mo. 5s.

Cicero, Part III.; containing the Tusculan Disputations (entire). With English Notes from Tischer, by the Rev. Archdeacon Paul. Second Edition. 5s. 6d.

Cicero, Part IV.; containing De Finibus Malorum et Bonorum. (On the Supreme Good.) With a Preface, English Notes, &c., partly from Madvig and others, by the Rev. James Beaven, D.D., late Professor of Theology in King's College, Toronto. 12mo. 5s. 6d.

ARNOLD'S SCHOOL SERIES. 23

Cicero, Part V.; containing Cato Major, sive De Senectute
Dialogus; with English Notes from Sommerbrodt, by the Rev. Henry
Browne, M.A., Canon of Chichester. 12mo. 2s. 6d.

Homer for Beginners.—The First Three Books of the Iliad,
with English Notes; forming a sufficient Commentary for Young Students.
Third Edition. 12mo. 3s. 6d.

Homer.—The Iliad Complete, with English Notes and
Grammatical References. Third Edition. In one thick volume, 12mo.
half-bound. 12s.

In this Edition, the Argument of each Book is divided into short Sections, which are prefixed to those portions of the Text, respectively, which they describe. The Notes (principally from Dübner) are at the foot of each page. At the end of the volume are useful Appendices.

Homer.—The Iliad, Books I. to IV.; with a Critical Introduction, and copious English Notes. Second Edition. 12mo. 7s. 6d.

Demosthenes, with English Notes from the best and most
recent sources, Sauppe, Doberenz, Jacobs, Dissen, Westermann, &c.
The Olynthiac Orations. Second Edition. 12mo. 3s.
The Oration on the Crown. Second Edition. 12mo. 4s. 6d.
The Philippic Orations. Second Edition. 12mo. 4s.

Æschines.—Speech against Ctesiphon. 12mo. 4s.

The Text is that of *Baiter* and *Sauppe*; the Notes are by Professor
Champlin, with additional Notes by President Woolsey and the Editor.

Sophocles, with English Notes, from Schneidewin. By the
Ven. Archdeacon Paul, and the Rev. Henry Browne, M.A.
The Ajax. 3s.—The Philoctetes. 3s.—The Œdipus Tyrannus. 4s.—
The Œdipus Coloneus. 4s.—The Antigone. 4s.

Euripides, with English Notes, from Hartung, Dübner,
Witzschel, Schöne, &c.
The Hecuba.—The Hippolytus.—The Bacchæ.—The Medea.—The
Iphigenia in Tauris, 3s. *each.*

Aristophanes.—Eclogæ Aristophanicæ, with English Notes,
by Professor Felton. Part I. (The Clouds.) 12mo. 3s. 6d. Part II.
(The Birds.) 3s. 6d.

⁎ *In this Edition the objectionable passages are omitted.*

A Descriptive Catalogue of the whole of Arnold's School
Series, may be had gratis.
Also, Rivington's complete Classified School Catalogue.

Publishing Monthly, price 1s.

The Englishman's Magazine

OF

LITERATURE, RELIGION, SCIENCE, AND ART.

Contents of No. 10, for October, 1865.

1. THE SEA-SIDE. *By George Tugwell, M.A., Author of "A Manual of the Sea Anemones."* II. Down among the Tangles.
2. HARVEST HOME.
3. STRAY THOUGHTS ON FAILURES.
4. SOME ACCOUNT OF BARRACK-LIFE IN INDIA. *By an Officer there.*
5. CANTERBURY AND THE PRIMATES.
6. THE ORPHAN CHORISTER.
7. THE OLD PAGODA TREE. A Story in Five Parts. *By Iltudus T. Prichard, Author of "How to Manage it," "Mutinies in Rajpootana," &c.*
    Part III. Chapter VII.—A Friend in Need.
    Chapter VIII.—The Temple-cave.
    Chapter IX.—Captivity.
8. THE POWER OF THOUGHT. *Imitated from Calderon. By Archdeacon Churton.*
9. MAN BEFORE HISTORY. *By T. G. Bonney, M.A., F.G.S.* II. The Lakes, Shores, and Morasses.
10. "WE ARE."
11. ST. CHARLES BORROMEO.
12. RENDERINGS FROM THE GERMAN.—Song of Liberty.—The Night Ride.

RIVINGTONS,
LONDON, OXFORD, AND CAMBRIDGE.

www.ingramcontent.com/pod-product-compliance
Lightning Source LLC
Chambersburg PA
CBHW020824230426
43666CB00007B/1095